The Contributors

Ronald Arnold   A member of Her Majesty's Inspectorate of Schools

Edwin Cox   Reader in Religious Education, University of London Institute of Education

Tom Dodd   Adviser to the Manpower Services Commission

Denis Lawton   Professor of Education and Director, University of London Institute of Education

Jon Ogborn   Professor of Science Education, University of London Institute of Education

Ken Robinson   Editor, *Arts Express*, and a contributor to the Gulbenkian report on arts education

Linda Thomas   Joint Secretary, Economics Research and Curriculum Unit, University of London Institute of Education

Lionel Ward   Lecturer in Education, University College of Swansea

Richard Whitburn   Inspector for Social Sciences, Inner London Education Authority at the time of writing his paper

Foreword

In recent years there has been a good deal of discussion about the need for every school to plan its own curriculum, bearing in mind national guidelines. In some respects, this need is self-evident, but many teachers complain about the enormous gap between the kind of principles and generalisations which would be acceptable nationally, and the kind of planning that goes on at the level of the individual teacher planning a series of lessons.

To meet the demand for some kind of 'middle ground' curriculum planning, the Centre for Teachers at the University of London Institute of Education organised a conference at which eight subject or area curriculum specialists were given the opportunity to outline what they felt should comprise a common curriculum. At the end of the conference many teachers expressed the hope that there would be some kind of permanent record of the conference in a form which would help others in the task of school-based curriculum planning. This book is the result of the invitation to the participants to rewrite their original papers.

The problem with any set of national aims or guidelines is that they tend to be acceptable only so long as they refrain from too much detail. But the practising teacher needs to plan in considerable detail. A further difficulty is that there is a variety of competing models available at national level. Apparently not even DES officials and Her Majesty's Inspectors can agree on a common model. Should teachers accept the views set out in *The Organisation and Content of the 5–16 Curriculum* or is the HMI 'areas of experience' model better? If so, why? In the first chapter of this book I will attempt to offer some guidance on that issue and put forward an alternative approach to curriculum planning based on cultural analysis. That introductory chapter will be followed by more detailed discussion and suggestions from the eight specialists. Each of these contributions could stand on its own as a useful contribution to curriculum planning, but in order to try to achieve some coherence for the book as a whole, I will introduce each of them with some further linking comments.

Finally, at the end of the book I will make some brief suggestions about how these 'theoretical' views might be put into practice by members of staff in a particular school.

Denis Lawton

School Curriculum Planning

Edited by
Denis Lawton

HODDER AND STOUGHTON

LONDON   SYDNEY   AUCKLAND   TORONTO

d642 6.86

British Library Cataloguing in Publication Data

School curriculum planning.——(Studies in teaching
   and learning)
   1. Curriculum planning——Great Britain
   I. Title   II. Series
   375′.001′0941   LB1564.G7

ISBN 0 340 38249 X

First published 1986

Printed in Great Britain for
Hodder and Stoughton Educational,
a division of Hodder and Stoughton Ltd,
Mill Road, Dunton Green, Sevenoaks, Kent,
by Richard Clay (The Chaucer Press) Ltd
Bungay, Suffolk

Contents

Studies in Teaching and Learning

The purpose of this series of short books on education is to make available readable, up-to-date views on educational issues and controversies. Its aim will be to provide teachers and students (and perhaps parents and governors) with a series of books which will introduce those educational topics which any intelligent and professional educationist ought to be familiar with. One of the criticisms levelled against 'teacher-education' is that there is so little agreement about what ground should be covered in courses at various levels; one assumption behind this series of texts is that there is a common core of knowledge and skills that all teachers need to be aware of, and the series is designed to map out this territory.

Although the major intention of the series is to provide general coverage, each volume will consist of more than a review of the relevant literature; the individual authors will be encouraged to give their own personal interpretation of the field and the way it is developing.

1 Cultural Analysis and Curriculum Planning

Denis Lawton

Most writers on curriculum over the last fifteen years or so have agreed that subjects will not do as the basis for curriculum planning. Subjects may well be used as part of the end product – the teaching programme of the school – but it is not appropriate to start with subjects. A prior question about the curriculum is what we want it for. In other words, we cannot talk sensibly about curriculum planning without engaging in debate about the purpose of education.

One of the criticisms made by HMI about school curricula in their primary and secondary surveys has been that the curriculum tends to lack balance. The same point has been made by DES writers on the curriculum and by many others. But Robert Dearden (1981) makes an interesting point about the use of the concept 'balance' in connection with the curriculum. Just as a balanced diet is assumed to be good, so is a balanced curriculum. Dearden, however, suggests that although the analogy may appear to be useful, we should look at it very carefully. One of the problems is that whereas the idea of a balanced diet rests on well established scientific data about vitamins, proteins, carbohydrates, minerals and so on, there is no such agreement about the ingredients in a balanced curriculum. The point that Dearden has made is that discussion of a balanced curriculum is meaningless unless there is some kind of prior commitment to the ingredients of the curriculum. No such prior commitment is spelt out either in DES documents such as *The School Curriculum* (1981a) or by Her Majesty's Inspectors in *A View of the Curriculum* (1980a) or *The Curriculum from 5 to 16* (1985).

The view of curriculum planning contained in this book is based on a prior commitment to education as a process of transmitting culture from one generation to the next. Culture in this context means, of course, not high culture (which would beg the question completely), but everything that is man-made in society: tools and technology, language and literature, music and art, science and mathematics, attitudes and values – the whole way of life of a society.

The first stage in this process of cultural analysis to establish what features or cultural systems every society, at any time or place, would necessarily possess. Elsewhere (Lawton, 1983) I have set out the reasons for stating that any society worthy of the title would need to have certain characteristics which could be sub-divided into eight cultural systems:

1 a socio-political system
2 an economic system
3 a communication system
4 a rationality system
5 a technology system
6 a morality system
7 a belief system
8 an aesthetic system

These eight systems are also justified empirically by the fact that no anthropologist has yet found any group of people living in a society without all of these features. The word 'society' might therefore be defined as a group of people living together and sharing at least those aspects of culture set out as eight 'systems'.

1 Socio-political System

Every society has some kind of system of defining relationships within the society as a whole. Kinship, status, role, duty and obligation, are some of the key socio-political concepts. In some societies, social structure is simple; in others, it is extremely complex and changeable. But a system of some kind will always exist.

2 Economic System

Every society has some means of dealing with the problem of distributing and exchanging scarce resources. Once again, societies will range from those where economic arrangements are extremely simple, to those where the system is so complex that few will understand it.

3 Communication System

In all societies human beings communicate with each other. One of the major differences between human beings and other animals is the existence of language. But an important feature which separates societies is the development of writing, and sometimes of print. These are of very great significance because the existence of print makes specialised knowledge more available, but at the same time encourages the tendency for specialisation, and therefore division in society.

4 Rationality System

All societies are rational in the sense of having a view about what is 'reasonable' and what counts as an explanation. The kinds of explanation may differ from time to time and place to place, but attempts are always made to explain physical phenomena and human behaviour. This system of rationality is closely linked with the communication system discussed above. Words and other signs must be used consistently to make comprehension and cooperation possible. One of the problems of modern industrial societies is that the rationality system may lack unity. This in itself presents additional problems in the educational process.

5 Technology System

Human beings in all societies have developed tools to build shelter from the climate, to produce food and to improve the quality of life in other ways. All human beings are 'technologists' in the sense of being users and makers of tools. The process of learning to use tools is an important feature of cultural life in all societies.

However, the system of technology may be so simple that every member of a society can master it, or so complex that no one individual could possibly understand all of it. Once again, the complexity of the technology system not only poses problems for cultural transmission, but also makes it necessary for decisions to be made in the educational system for general knowledge on the one hand, and specialisation on the other.

6 Morality System

All human beings are 'moral' animals. All societies have some kind of code of behaviour and make distinctions between right and wrong behaviour. What is regarded as appropriate in one society may be very different from the rules operating in another place or time, but there will always be some kind of moral system. The problem of passing on the morality system from one generation to the next is, however, much more difficult in a society where there are conflicting rules between sub-groups within that society, and possibly lack of clarity as to what the moral code really is.

7 Belief System

Any society will have some kind of dominant belief system. In some societies beliefs are predominantly of a religious kind, perhaps based on divine revelation. In other societies beliefs may be derived from myths about creation. In western industrial societies the religious beliefs have weakened to some extent and societies have become secularised. The belief system then tends to be a mixture of scientific or pseudo-scientific explanations, political beliefs and attempts to popularise various approaches to rational behaviour.

8 Aesthetic System

All human beings have aesthetic drives and needs: all societies produce some kind of art and entertainment for members of that society. In all cases, art has standards of form and substance, related to the value system, technology and social structure of that society. One of the problems, however, is that as the social, political and economic structures become more complex, so do the rules of aesthetic criteria become more difficult to specify. Whereas aesthetic tastes and their underlying criteria in a simple society can be passed on automatically from one generation to the next, in a more complex industrialised society the rapid rate of change of aesthetic tastes makes it difficult to establish, and to transmit acceptable standards in the educational process. Nevertheless, these are duties which schools cannot avoid.

Having described these eight cultural systems in general – that is, as they apply in principle to any society – the next stage in the process of cultural analysis would be to apply each of those cultural systems to one particular society. Then the third step would be to derive from the description of each cultural system in one society (Britain), a reasonable curriculum for that society today. This would be an example of curriculum planning being based on a selection from the culture of a given society. Such a curriculum would have something in common with any other national curriculum, but the differences would be extremely interesting and important.

This was the task set for each of our eight curriculum experts. In most cases they are assuming that the reader already has a good deal of knowledge about the particular cultural system under discussion. In each case, however, I will – at the risk of stating the obvious – make a few introductory points about that particular cultural system in Britain today.

Part of the reason for adopting a cultural analysis approach is that curriculum theorisers have frequently pointed out that one of the dangers of any school system is that it tends to lag behind the changing culture in a variety of ways. The process of cultural lag and curriculum inertia has often been discussed in general terms, but it is also useful to try and pin-point gaps in the existing curriculum to identify mismatches between what is and what ought to be, as well as trying to detect basic contradictions between what the belief system would say is important and what actually happens in most schools. That too will be part of the process of cultural analysis and curriculum planning.

2 The Socio-political System

Richard Whitburn

Introduction

The socio-political system might be regarded as one of the major casualties of curriculum planning. When we look at the complexity of the social structure in England, the vast network of social institutions and the historical development of political parties and other political groups, it is easy to see why many adults find it difficult to understand how their own society really works. But schools do very little to ensure that young people acquire even an elementary set of social and political concepts, let alone adequate social and political experiences. The problem has been regarded as critical by many observers, and when the Hansard Society made a survey of school leavers they entitled the report *A Study of 'Political Ignorance'*.

Some conventional subjects in the school curriculum such as history and geography, deal with some aspects of the socio-political structure, but as Richard Whitburn will point out, what ought to be on offer is much more complex and demanding.

Denis Lawton

Curriculum discussions often focus on the inadequacy of the subject-based curriculum, the historic palimpsest which in many ways stifles the capacity of schools to provide curriculum experiences which are appropriate and applicable to all pupils in the five years of compulsory secondary education. There have been many who have questioned the status quo in curriculum terms and offered theoretical and radical proposals for change, but the practical realisation of such proposals is less evident. As Professor Lawton has suggested in his cultural analysis approach to curriculum planning, there needs to be an underlying perception of the aims of schooling, and based on that a re-evaluation of the curriculum to establish the degree to which the present offering, or any new proposal, actually achieves these aims. In the cultural model the concern is to transmit certain elements of culture to the next generation, based on an analysis of the essential elements of culture to which every child should have access.

In recent years there have been a number of proposals concerning the structure of the curriculum each of which has identified some area of human/social studies. Professor Lawton (Skilbeck, 1984) identifies the area as the socio-political system:

> All societies have some kind of social structure, some kind of system of defining relationships within society as a whole. Kinship, status, role, duty and obligation are key social concepts which not only exist in every society, but need to be passed on to the next generation. In some societies the social structure is simple, taken for granted, in others the social structure is complex, open to debate and possible change.

If we accept this analysis of curriculum which involves areas of experience and identifies the socio-political as one of those areas, then we need to answer basic questions:

What do we consider to be the socio-political?
What is the irreducible minimum which we would expect such a curriculum to contain?
How do we achieve such a curriculum in practice?

It is important to recognise initially that the school curriculum can be examined in a number of different ways, each of which has significance in terms of the provision of social and political education. There is the formal timetabled curriculum which reflects the traditional subject-divided, planned instructional activities of the school in an academic sense. There is a wider interpretation of all of the planned learning intentions of the staff, which would include formal lessons and also the whole range of planned activities including clubs, visits and other organised activities out of school. There is also that aspect of school life which includes everything which takes place within a school that results in learning whether intended or not – the 'hidden curriculum'. Nowhere is this more significant than in the area of social and political education.

Traditionally, the development of social and political understanding has found a place in examinable courses – government and politics, social studies, geography, economics, history – most of which will have been open only to senior pupils. There has, until recently, been no general understanding that knowledge, skills and concepts concerning the social and political should form part of the curriculum for all pupils. That is not to say, however, that the timetable should necessarily include a separate, identifiable additional subject on the curriculum entitled social or political education, although that is a possibility. Many other subjects can and do make a contribution to the development of young people's social and political competence. However, it is important to be clear that such practice is understood and recognised to be part of a planned programme of work undertaken by the school, the department and the teacher in social and political education.

Quite clearly the role of whole school policies towards children's learning, to language development, to number work, to knowledge, skills, attitudes and concepts, to assessment and evaluation, to the reflection of and valuing of the wider community and towards such fundamental issues as racism and gender, are crucial in the development of a programme of work designed to develop social and political understanding.

It would be impossible and inappropriate to recount the detailed history of work in this area over the years. However, it is worthwhile considering some of the work which has been undertaken which has increasingly influenced and put pressure on the traditional school curriculum. In terms of the provision and growth of social and political education, it was an aspect of the curriculum which hardly existed, certainly as an identifiable area, in most schools twenty years ago. Today there is a considerable volume of practice which has experienced swift growth in the last fifteen years. Purely in examination terms it is a field which currently offers in excess of 100,000 candidates at 16+ for either CSE or O level.

Why such a growth? Undoubtedly the raising of the school leaving age in 1972 gave a tremendous impetus to school curriculum discussions, particularly in terms of the relationship between the child's experience in school and in society. There was an increasing concern for 'relevance' in the curriculum and a desire to see education better preparing young people for 'adult and working life' – in an active participative manner. At the same time the growth in the social sciences in higher education resulted in an increasing number of social science graduates entering teaching and concerned to contribute their subject to children's education.

Social and political education was beginning to emerge in its present form in schools at the same time as the Schools Council began generating its major curriculum projects. The range and variety of the curriculum work undertaken by the Schools Council was impressive. Much of their innovative classroom practice and emphasis on new approaches and materials was readily adopted and adapted by a receptive audience of teachers developing courses in the social/political area, where there were no preconceived models of traditional and acceptable practice. Teachers were also often dealing with pupils who had been disaffected by the traditional curriculum experience and methods of schooling, and for whom discussion, enquiry, and the opportunity to examine the contemporary and draw on their own experience were very positive motivating factors. It is appropriate to draw attention here to the work undertaken by the Humanities Curriculum Project under the direction of the late Lawrence Stenhouse and his team at East Anglia University. Whilst in many ways that project has faded into curriculum history, its lessons and experience abound in the understanding and awareness of the appropriateness and importance of discussion based on evidence, and of the need to address fundamental and controversial issues in the classroom.

The extension of the franchise to 18 year olds brought into sharp focus the degree to which the education provided in our schools afforded a sound basis for choice on the part of the newly enfranchised youth. At the same time teachers and others involved in education had been exploring practical ways in which political education could become a reality in schools. The establishment of the Politics Association in 1969, the publication of the Hansard Society's *Programme for Political Education* in 1978 with its concern to develop 'political literacy' in secondary schools, the publication of the HMI discussion document on 'Political Competence' in 'The Red Book' (*Curriculum 11–16*, 1977) and the range of subsequent developments at universities and schools throughout the country have maintained and informed the curriculum discussion on political education.

Interest has also stemmed from a concern variously expressed in recent documents on the school curriculum from the DES, HMI and

LEA Advisory/Inspectorate teams that education should provide the means whereby young people can understand and participate actively in adult society at a local, national and international level. The statement of the aims of education which is contained in the Warnock Report (1978) is typical:

> First, to enlarge a child's knowledge, experience and imaginative understanding, and thus his awareness of moral values and capacity for enjoyment; and secondly, to enable him to enter the world after formal education is over as an active participant in society and a responsible contributor to it, capable of achieving as much independence as possible.

Social Education

In many ways the aims identified by the Schools Council in *The Practical Curriculum* (1981) reflect the overall character of social education in its widest definition.

> Schools have the capacity and the will to help their pupils in at least six ways:
> 1 to acquire knowledge, skills and practical abilities and the will to use them;
> 2 to develop qualities of mind, body, spirit, feeling and imagination;
> 3 to appreciate human achievements in art, music, science, technology and literature;
> 4 to acquire understanding of the social, economic and political order, and a reasoned set of attitudes, values and beliefs;
> 5 to prepare for their adult lives at home, at work, at leisure and at large, as consumers and citizens; and most important of all;
> 6 to develop a sense of self respect, the capacity to live as independent, self-motivated adults and the ability to function as contributing members of co-operative groups.

It is quite clear that these aspects of social education are not the responsibility of one area within a school nor of a particular course, but are the responsibility of all those involved in the educational exercise of the school and are seen to be developed through the specific academic curriculum, the wider and pastoral curriculum of the school and in the hidden curriculum – that sum total of all of the formal and informal relationships, attitudes and values that are generated within a school and reflect in every aspect of the school's life.

Equally it is recognised that the social sciences have as their major concern the study of social life in all its forms throughout the world, and thus has an important contribution to make to the educational experience of all children. It is clearly not possible to present a total picture of social science knowledge of human societies, the ways in which those societies have been investigated, or the range of concepts used to organise information about them. Indeed it may well be that aspects of that knowledge are more appropriate than others to pupils' needs, maturity and abilities – and more relevant in terms of the development of their understanding of their own society. The selection of content from such a large potential reservoir is essential and the criteria on which such a selection is made should be clear.

There are a number of ways in which social science courses are developed and this is reflected in the diversity and range of Mode III courses in the social sciences. Whilst it may be helpful to identify a number of such approaches it will be recognised that none of these models is exclusive, most courses will involve elements of one or more of these approaches.

An approach based on methods of enquiry

A course may be developed on the basis of introducing children to the range of enquiry methods used by the social scientist to derive their knowledge of society. The emphasis in such a scheme is the development of the pupils' critical understanding of the way knowledge is derived. Pupils are encouraged to undertake studies themselves, to approach an issue in an open ended manner in order to understand the way particular conclusions have been reached. Particular issues or topics may be selected not because the content is especially relevant or important, but because they offer the opportunity to examine a range of methods and thus establish a number of generalisations concerning particular approaches.

An approach based on pupils' experience and interests

Certain schemes are designed to draw on the pupils' own experience and interests, thus bridging the gap between academic knowledge and everyday knowledge. They have the added attraction of identifying the subject more closely with the pupils' perceptions of relevance and importance. Clearly such an approach may result in the pursuit of a topic of great interest but relatively little inherent worth, and thus the role of the teacher in such a programme is a difficult and exacting one. Many well established courses of this type also have strong elements of the methods-based approach.

An approach based on concepts

A scheme may be designed to give pupils the opportunity to develop understandings of key ideas and concepts in the social sciences. Concepts which are capable of wide application and enable us all better to understand the social world. Such an approach emphasises the development of the students' thinking ability rather than the transmission of set bodies of 'knowledge'. Under such a scheme topics and issues are selected because they clearly exemplify particular concepts which are appropriate for the pupils at this stage in their development.

An approach based on content

Schemes based on content may be organised in a number of ways. Some content-based courses identify essential information, particular topics, themes or issues which include essential information, facts and knowledge about society which is regarded as an important element in the pupils' education. Inevitably there is content in all schemes which pupils undertake in schools, but the distinguishing feature of many courses based on such an approach is their identification of central, essential information, often of a very practical character, which it is deemed the pupil ought to know.

The following series of questions from ILEA's *History and Social Sciences at Secondary Level Part III Social Sciences* form a useful starting point in the consideration of the selection for such courses:

* Why do we feel an understanding of particular aspects of society is important for pupils to acquire?
* What do we want pupils to learn about society?
* How are we going to enable them to obtain relevant information and assess their understanding of society?
* How does this relate to the development of basic concepts, attitudes and skills?
* How are pupils going to make use of what they learn, both at the present time and in their future lives?

Political Education

The term political education is broad and capable of wide interpretation and misinterpretation; there is no generally accepted academic definition. There are those who define political education as the process of informing young people of basic political 'facts' – for instance, the philosophies and processes of local and central government. Few would question that it is important for all young people – indeed, all citizens – to acquire and possess this kind of knowledge. But many would argue that this is a limited view of political education and indeed of education as a whole. While confirming that political education should include the acquisition of political 'facts', they maintain that it must also involve the development of certain skills and attitudes which are necessary if pupils are to learn to participate fully in political processes. Essentially, according to the HMI (1977) document *Curriculum 11–16*, political education is:

> concerned with relationships in society: between individuals, between individuals and social groups, and between social groups. It involves a consideration of beliefs and values, of purposes and motivations, of rules and conventions, of authority and power. Understanding one's own personal relationships requires self-knowledge as well as knowledge of, and sensitivity towards, others.

The chief objection to political education comes from those who consider that the school curriculum should be 'neutral' and value-free, devoid of contentious issues. They feel that political education should be concerned primarily with imparting knowledge about parliamentary processes, and courses should be developed within a strictly defined parameter (Boyson, 1978):

> If it is to be introduced, then it should be included as a body of knowledge and should cover how local government works, how Parliament works, how the law courts work, the rule of law and the functions of the police.

However, such a viewpoint fails to acknowledge that there are certain fundamental values which determine the conduct of our society – values which the school curriculum must surely reflect if it is to prepare young people adequately for life after school. These are the values of an open society – one which accepts diversity of belief, encourages participation, and recognises the right of the individual to assess evidence and formulate his or her own position. Schools surely have an obligation to develop in young people the skills and knowledge which will equip them for informed and responsible political participation. Again HMI (1977):

> Those who claim that politics ought to be 'kept out of' whatever it may be are being ingenuous (or, on occasions, disingenuous and politically skilful). Wherever there is disagreement, there lies a potential for politics, for aggregating issues, organising support, arguing, propagat-

ing, settling difficulties. There is 'politics' in this wide sense in every club, society or classroom if we did but see it. Possibly those who are coy about 'politics' mean 'party politics', but British democracy is parliamentary and rests on national parties, which are inevitably enmeshed with major issues, a fact more readily understood by the politically literate.

Thus political education is concerned with areas of knowledge, skill and competence and with values and attitudes which underly the democratic system. In the same document HMI described the content of political education in the following manner:

First there must be an understanding of the machinery, not only of central and local government, but also industrial relations, the education system, and the contribution made by pressure groups. Second it must include an understanding of issues over which people disagree. Disagreements may be over goals (where we are going? what purpose would a given action serve?); or over results (what is the right outcome? the fairest? the best?). For young people aged 11 to 16 issues must be related to concrete examples, such as the Welfare State, motorways, comprehensive schools, capital punishment, abortion, strikes. Thirdly, there must be a knowledge of the groups that are involved in political decision making, e.g., political parties, trade unions, the CBI, the press and interest groups. It must examine the effect on political aspirations and the effectiveness of, for example, regional, economic and ethnic differences. In order to have some insights into these areas it is also necessary to see them in some historical perspective which will demonstrate not only the potential, but the limitations of political action.

Political education is also concerned with attitudes and values; attitudes such as open-mindedness, toleration, compromise; procedural values such as respect for truth and rationality; substantive values which form the basis of social life, the sanctity of life for example. Such attitudes and values require certain skills and abilities on the part of the pupils if they are to be developed. Pupils need to be able to find evidence, sift and evaluate it, identify bias, understand and appreciate the point of view of others, make decisions and argue their case. Such attitudes, values and skills are reflected in many aspects of the work of schools, but political education is concerned to encourage the pupils' active participation in society; it is not merely concerned to develop knowledge, attitudes, values and skills, but to enhance the pupils capacity for active participation. As Alex Porter (Crick and Porter, 1980) has pointed out:

. . . political literacy would be limited to a solitary intellectual exercise; the politically literate person would merely be capable of well-informed observation and analysis. The ultimate test of effective political education lies in creating a proclivity to action.

Teaching Approaches

There are various approaches which are adopted by teachers to develop programmes of work in social and political education. One of the great problems which confronts anyone engaged in teaching is the selection that is made for the pupils from the body of concepts, skills and knowledge which is available, and which forms the basis on which the disciplines of academic study are founded. Against the desirable balance of such concepts, skills and knowledge must be set the pupils' own needs and requirements, the perceptions and demands of society as a whole, and the reflection of those demands and requirements where appropriate through the public examination system. There is undoubtedly a tension between a strong academic orientation on the one hand, closely related to higher education perceptions of appropriate performance and results, and on the other hand a more practical view of the curriculum providing a survival pack for life in an increasingly sophisticated society. It would be naive to categorise responses quite so simplistically. The range is wide and the interweaving of various threads of differrent aims and philosophies into the current provision is complex.

Only a relatively small proportion of young people will pursue studies of the social and political at advanced academic higher education level, yet all will be concerned with such issues throughout their lives. Some schools recognise the importance of such studies to be such that they are accorded high status as part of the school's core curriculum. Alternatively, elements of such study are incorporated in a core course which might also include moral, health, sex and rights education, perhaps within the personal/pastoral curriculum of the school. Many formal pastoral curriculum programmes involve personality development and personal decision-making in which there is considerable development of skills important in social and political education.

Schools need to identify and plan the aims and objectives of their programmes of work which include social and political education. This involves examining particular areas of content, and certain concepts, skills and attitudes, which can be outlined, for example in terms of political education in the following way (ILEA, 1983).

Content

Pupils need to acquire
* an understanding of the issues over which people disagree – real issues, such as comprehensive education, industrial action, privatisation of medical care, nationalisation of industry, capital punishment, abortion. . .
* a knowledge of the groups involved in political decision-making – for instance, political parties, trade unions, the CBI, the press – and their respective roles
* an understanding of the processes and influence of local and central government in, for instance, industrial relations or the educational system, as well as the contribution of pressure groups.

Concepts

Pupils need to gain an understanding of the concepts used to categorise political knowledge and experience. Among these are:

* *general political concepts*
  such as power, authority, welfare, freedom, liberty
* *concepts associated with political machinery*
  such as elections, reform, pressure groups
* *concepts associated with beliefs and ideologies*
  such as socialism, communism, democracy, conservatis
* *concepts associated with specific issues*
  such as nationalism, devolution, pacifism, racism.

Attitudes

Attitudes which are fundamental to responsible political activity need to to be encouraged in pupils. These include:
* an awareness of the importance of politics in their lives
* an awareness and understanding of politics and society
* an interest and concern to participate and contribute to society
* tolerance – an acceptance and respect for the right of people to hold diverse views
* open-mindedness – a recognition of the value of healthy scepticism
* an acceptance of compromise – a willingness to look for ways in which disagreement can be resolved without force
* to foster a sense of personal responsibility for individual decisions and actions.

Skills

Certain skills are necessary for pupils to develop political competence, for instance, the ability to:

* seek, question and evaluate a range of views and evidence
* recognise slanted interpretation, exaggeration and bias
* distinguish between 'fact' and opinion
* recognise the reasons for the positions people adopt, and the effects of certain courses of action
* identify the choices open to them and establish the action they themselves wish to pursue
* enable pupils to express themselves politically.

Sir James Hamilton, formerly a Permanent Secretary of State at the DES stated (1982) his awareness of:

a growing consensus that the time is ripe to re-examine the secondary curriculum not just in terms of the traditional subject divisions and the knowledge and skills which can be imparted, but in terms of preparation for adult and working life defined more broadly.

Undoubtedly, schools have come under increasing pressure from a number of very different directions, reflecting a wide range of views as to what sort of 'adult and working life' the 1990s will present, and thus what forms of education will constitute sound preparation for such life.

There is a strong practical thrust in many of the arguments currently posed in terms of the development of 'basic skills' and courses of vocational preparation, which have come to the fore in the area of 16–19 provision and are now influencing the 11–16 curriculum. At the same time there is a growing recognition of the obligation schools have to enable young people to acquire a basic understanding of themselves and the society in which they live, and the necessary skills and attitudes to confidently participate and contribute in society. In order to implement such programmes schools will need to examine carefully what is currently provided as social and political education against the sort of criteria established above. They will also need to re-examine whole school policies in terms of teaching and learning strategies, assessment, and cross curriculum liaison and coordination. This may well result in a radical restructuring of the traditional organisation of teaching and learning into units or modules of work from first to fifth year, involving core units which may be integrated, subject- or skills-based. Such units are unlikely to be continuous throughout the five years, but would be likely to accord more appropriately with knowledge of the way young people learn best. Implicit in such a reorganisation would be the possibility of some flexibility in the examining process and a questioning of what constitutes appropriate preparation for public examination.

3 The Economic System

Linda Thomas

Introduction

Dr Linda Thomas, throughout her chapter, discusses the needs of pupils in terms of 'economic literacy', just as many writers (such as Crick and Porter) have used the term 'political literacy'. It is a useful approach which has at least two advantages. First, it makes the sensible assumption that everyone should be literate; second, it begins to spell out what it is that anyone would need to know, what skills to possess, in order to be considered economically literate. In other words, underlying the concept 'literacy' (whether it is political literacy or economic or any other) is a concept of a common culture and a common curriculum.

Linda Thomas has herself made significant contributions to the definition of economic literacy, not least in her PhD thesis (1981), which is referred to in the chapter which follows.

Denis Lawton

This chapter is concerned with the introduction into schools of programmes designed to promote economic literacy in all students. The first section argues that the case for economic literacy programmes is overwhelming because it is derived from the nature of the economic system itself, and from the unique contribution which an insight into economics makes to the education of young people. In the second section an attempt is made to translate the argument into a working definition of economic literacy. In the third section the implications of this view for curriculum planning are analysed in the context of present day curricular constraints and developments. A fourth section provides examples of materials, approaches and resources which incorporate the definition of economic literacy developed here, and which are available to help schools who are tackling the problem of introducing an economic literacy element into the curriculum.

The Economic System and the Role of Economics

The Green Paper, *Education in Schools: A Consultative Document* (DES, 1977a) lists as one of the eight major curricular aims:

> to help children to appreciate how a nation earns and maintains its standard of living, and properly to estimate the essential role of industry and commerce in this process.

This position is justified by pointing out that:

> only a minority of schools convey adequately to their pupils the fact that ours is an industrial society in a mixed economy.

The DES (1977b) document *Curriculum 11–16*, prepared by the HMI Curriculum Review Group, states that:

> Given the nature of the industrial society in which we must live, no one questions the crucial importance of 'economic competence' for all citizens. This competence should be enjoyed, as far as is realistically possible, by every sixteen year old.

The DES (1980b) publication *A Framework for the School Curriculum* also pointed out that:

> Schools contribute to the preparation of young people for all aspects of adult life . . . . substantial attention should be given at the secondary

stage to the relationship between school work and preparation for working life. Pupils need to acquire an understanding of the economic basis of society and how wealth is created.

The Schools Council (1981) includes as one of its six general recommendations in *The Practical Curriculum* that schools should help pupils:

to acquire understanding of the social, economic and political order.

More recently the DES (1982b) document *17+: A New Qualification* states that the common activities which should occupy students for 60 % of their time must include studies designed to give a broad understanding of the way in which the country earns its living. And the concern recently expressed by Sir Keith Joseph, Secretary of State for Education and Science, that pupils should 'acquire knowledge of the economic foundation of society' and be made aware of 'the economic facts of life' is but the latest example of this public concern.

The argument developed by Professor Lawton in Chapter 1 provides a theoretical basis for the increase in public interest, illustrated above, in the provision of some aspects of economic understanding in the curriculum because it justifies from a cultural analysis perspective some study of the economic system. A cursory examination of the nature of the economic system and of its influence on individuals and groups in our nation is sufficient to demonstrate its validity.

The economic system is the means whereby scarce resources are transformed into things which meet the country's needs. It is a decisive element in the social, cultural and political framework of the nation; it is embodied in institutions, mechanisms, techniques and conventions and finds expression in constraints, policies, habits, motivations and values. Ultimately its existence depends upon the presence of scarcity and the resulting need to mitigate the effects of the constraints scarcity imposes on individual choice. Paradoxically, the economic system itself creates further constraints on choice. For example, it is possible to perceive the difference between the two photographs (over) as a representation of the effect of scarcity. Alternatively, it is possible to argue that they give the lie to the notion of 'pure' scarcity and confront us with the realities of economic life and the power possessed by the economic system both to constrain choice and to influence behaviour.

Courtesy of Oxfam – Kurigram Children's Feeding Centre, 1974.

Courtesy of Manchester University.

The 'economic facts of life' seem therefore to be uncomplicated:

The economic system exerts an influence on individual behaviour
Individuals play a part in and make a contribution to the
economic system
The economic system is neither static nor sacrosanct
Individual and group behaviour can have an important effect on
the development of the economic system

It is possible to argue that only those who grasp these economic
facts – the meaning of the part they play in the system, the nature of
their individual contribution and its effect upon the system – can be
expected to cope constructively with its power and influence. If this
is so, our students are entitled to expect the educational system to
provide them with the means to attain that position. Economics
education has a crucial role to play in this process, since it is only
through an economics perspective that students can achieve
sufficient objectivity to ensure a realistic scrutiny and evaluation of
the economic issues, problems, experiences and policies that
confront individuals and nations.

Economists are concerned to explain how the economic system
works, but the power of economics' contribution to the general
education of young people lies not in the economists' search for
greater accuracy and precision, but in the provision of a theoretical
framework which they can use to organise information and reflect on
experience, and which ultimately gives access to the economics
perspective. It is possible to *comprehend* statements made by indus-
trialists, union leaders, politicians and newspaper journalists without an economics perspective; and to *describe* the choices made by
individuals and corporations. An economics perspective however
provides the means to *analyse* and *evaluate* them. Indeed, without an
economics perspective – the means for objective analysis of particular situations and experiences – day-by-day experiences of the
economic system both in ordinary life and through carefully
constructed curricular activities may never be properly understood.
Instead it may merely foster or reinforce misconceptions and
prejudice.

My own research study (Thomas, 1981) provided some evidence
to support this claim. For example, in reply to a question on the
effect of changes in demand and supply on prices, 80% of the
answers given by two hundred and thirty four 12–16 year old pupils,
while seeming to be extremely varied in character, showed that the
majority of this sample of pupils saw price as an instrument
controlled by the suppliers of goods and used by them to protect or

improve their present levels of income. This conceptualisation allowed pupils to support a variety of arguments such as the following: an increase in supply could result in bulk buying and a reduction in costs and therefore a reduction in price would not endanger income levels; an increase in demand would allow an improvement in income levels; an increase in supply could result in increased costs and therefore an increase in price would be necessary to protect income levels. In this case experiences of a wide range of different markets merely fostered naive and unhelpful misconceptions both about the economic system's influence and the effects of the actions of individuals.

In practice what this means is that it is perfectly feasible for programmes of activity to require students to conduct surveys, to handle information, to list functions, to identify organisations, to use appropriate terminology, to distinguish between different types of institutions[1] and thus appear to be providing opportunities for increasing understanding, whereas in reality they merely represent a descriptive, information gathering process. It is also possible for programmes of activity to require students to group phenomena, to draw comparisons, to investigate relationships and links which may be perceived within the economic environment, to contruct models, and thus to appear to be contributing to the development of a framework of theory by providing opportunities for conceptualisation, whereas in reality students learn labels and manipulate given categories. It is possible for programmes of activity to require students to coordinate data, to manipulate economic variables, to defend opinions and decisions, to check, plan, budget and calculate, and thus to appear to be contributing to the development of analytical and procedural skills, whereas in reality they merely offer opportunities to practice non-transferable skills. Lastly, it is possible for programmes of activity to require students to investigate important economic issues, and thus appear to be contributing to economics education, whereas they merely invite emotional and subjective responses. The difference between the two outcomes is one of perspective.

Towards a Working Definition of Economic Literacy

It has been argued above that young people have a right of access to the means for objective analysis, an economics perspective, and with it the foundation for developing a critical awareness of the way the economic system works. This may be envisaged in the form of a set of aims.

Aims of Economic Literacy Programmes

- to help young people to understand their own economic experience and thus to appreciate their relationship with the economic system, the importance of their personal contribution to that system and the strength of its influence on their lives.

- to help young people to develop a critical awareness of the way the economic system works.

It has also been argued that access to the economics perspective – the means for objective analysis of particular situations, experiences and economic policies which involve a choice in the use of scarce resources – is derived from the use of a general theoretical framework to organise information and reflect on experience. In other words, the economics perspective originates in the theory that:

> choice behaviour is constrained by scarcity and the influence of the economic system. The opportunity costs for the individual and the real costs to society of any choice behaviour involving the use of scarce resources at the margin are not reflected by prices or money costs.

This statement defines the theoretical framework of economics. It may be represented, in operational form, as a procedural framework which exemplifies the application of the general concepts of opportunity cost, marginality and efficiency to analyses of particular situations, and which allows the theoretical framework to operate as a means of organising information and reflecting on experience. This procedural framework takes the following form:

Procedural Framework for Economic Literacy

- Examine any marginal decision involving the use of scarce resources. Deduce whether the decision indicates that marginal benefits are greater than or equal to prices or money costs.

- Does it represent the best use of scarce resources? What does best mean?

- Are any costs other than money involved? Analyse the question in opportunity cost terms: 1 What returns are available from alternative uses of the resources? 2 What other resource use is involved as a result of the decision? 3 Are external/social costs present?

- Re-examine the choice behaviour. Consider benefits at the margin in relation to costs at the margin noting the effect of value judgments.

- Does it represent the best use of scarce resources? What does best mean?

- Consider policy implications.

- Alternatively, start with a policy or advisory statement and work backwards, exposing the value judgment involved.

This procedural framework forms the basis for developing a critical awareness of the way the economic system works because it provides access to an economics perspective. It is recognisable in any valid piece of economic reasoning at any level.[2]

Economic literacy programmes in the 14–18 curriculum should be clearly identified with such a procedural framework, for it permits students to consider experience and/or problems involving a choice in the use of resources in the real world in a particular and aware way. Instead of transmitting a received view of the economic system, such programmes will provide access to an economics perspective by allowing the necessary procedures to be appropriated by constant use. Moreover, they will encourage the development of the intellectual, procedural and practical skills which are necessary to handle information, coordinate data, explore relationships, form concepts, etc.

Individuals who are economically literate are able to use these skills within the procedural framework of economics to comprehend in their own terms the concepts (e.g. scarcity and choice, supply, demand, etc.) used by economists to define those relationships in the economic system which are of interest to them. They are also able to use these skills to generate an objective and dynamic base of information. Thus, individuals who are economically literate are empowered to act confidently in the complex modern world not only as informed but also as competent consumers, producers and citizens.

The objectives of economic literacy programmes may therefore be summarised as follows:

The Economic Perspective

Economic literacy programmes should require students to view situations and experiences which necessitate choice in an economic way – by means of its key concepts – and to reflect on their own experiences by means of an economics rather than a descriptive approach, so that they are given the opportunity to:
- be realistic and objective;
- become aware of misconceptions formed as a result of early economics experiences;
- distinguish between facts and values;
- recognise the use of economic power.

> ### The Economics Perspective
>
> The use of a procedural framework derived from theory as a means of analysis – to determine which variables are relevant and to provide a means of evaluating information about the variables.

Skills

In doing so they will encourage the development of intellectual, procedural and practical skills:
- so that students can develop enough confidence (as well as information, knowledge and understanding) to act in the complex world as competent consumers and producers.

> ### Examples
>
> Handling simple data and statistics; where to go for information; processing data, translating it from one form to another and using it to support arguments and points of view; organising and presenting economic ideas.

Conceptual Development

Economic literacy programmes which satisfy the objectives will also allow students to conceptualise – that is, to explore relationships and interconnections – so that they can:

> ### Examples of Economic Concepts and Principles
>
> The role and importance of industry and institutions; the differences between wealth, value added and income; the

- use the concepts which are used by economists to classify experience and describe relationships;
- gain some idea of how the economic system works, not only how institutions work;
- correct any early misconceptions.

Information

They will also help to provide an adequate information base:
- so that students are able to identify the terms which are used on forms and in newspapers and television reports, and can act as informed citizens in our society.

effects of government; the relationship of the parts to the whole; the consequences of changing technology for firms, industries and employment; the links between money incomes, changing prices and living standards.

Examples

The meanings of terms in common use in economics such as banks, balance of payments, exports, etc; the characteristics and function of institutions such as trades unions, VAT, etc; particular aspects of the system which bear on our lives such as how prices are arrived at, how wages and other sector prices are determined, the role of money, etc.

Curriculum Planning

If all young people are entitled to the knowledge, information and skills which will enable them to understand the salient features of the economic environment in which they live – that is, to be economically literate – and if it is education's responsibility to make that knowledge and know-how accessible in a coherent form, the programmes which are made available to every student as part of the general curriculum must reflect that responsibility. This is the problem facing curriculum designers.

Schools, however, also operate within the economic system and are subject to constraints which restrict range of choice and which influence the decisions they make. Some of the constraints which may affect the introduction of economic literacy programmes in particular are the need to accommodate students of all ability, teachers with no formal economics training, the pressure on curriculum time from existing courses and new developments, and the existence of a prescriptive examination system. Any suggested solution to the curriculum design problem will therefore be evaluated in terms of its ability to obviate such constraints.

It is possible to argue that the scheme, developed in the last section to give practical expression to the slogan 'economic literacy for all', does have the power to liberate curriculum planners from the influence of these constraints. Access to an economics perspective is provided by the use of a procedural framework to explore situations that have developed out of resource scarcity. The procedural framework is intelligible and comprehensive. It finds application in any circumstance, simple and complex, which involves a choice in the use of scarce resources. It is sufficiently robust to prepare students for economics at 16+ and in the CPVE; all students are able to appreciate its power in terms of their own experiences and in terms of their ability to understand, predict and explain the behaviour of the economic system; it may be used to provide a different dimension to the analysis of situations which originate in a range of curricular contexts. The issue of the allocation of scarce resources permeates into many subject areas, which thus provide opportunities for the application of the procedural framework and the development of skills and knowledge.

The topic of health may be considered in home economics, biology, PE and history lessons. It is possible to add an economic literacy dimension to the exercises if students are allowed to consider the full implications of choice and policy decisions. For example, the procedural framework can be used to analyse and evaluate smoking:

Economic Reasoning[3]

- Examine the decision to smoke one cigarette. Deduce whether it indicates that satisfaction is greater than or equal to money costs

- Does this decision represent the best use of scarce resources?

- Are any costs other than money involved? Analyse the question in opportunity cost terms.
    1 What other resource use is involved? What are the effects of smoking on health?
    2 Are external/social costs present?

> – Is satisfaction equal to real costs at the margin?
>
> – Does the decision represent the best use of resources? What does best mean?
>
> – What are the policy implications? Why is smoking not banned?

This procedure could also be used by PE departments to provide a new perspective on exercise. Students' work on diets in science or home economics provides opportunities to apply the same framework to an analysis of the real costs of government intervention in the food processing industry.

It is possible to give a different orientation to a great deal of scientific study, especially in areas concerned with ergonomics and the social and environmental effects of science, by means of an economics perspective.

Furthermore money management, industrial studies, careers and social studies courses frequently focus on choices which involve the allocation of scarce resources. They therefore provide an appropriate context for the inclusion of an economics education element.

This means that it is feasible for all schools to introduce an economic literacy element into the general curriculum for all students. Economic literacy programmes as defined here are not concerned to cover a bewildering mass of indigestible information, or to transmit diluted versions of A level economics models which have very little meaning for most 16 year old students. Instead they seek to add a new dimension to much of the work which is already being undertaken in schools, and to work through skills for living, personal and social development, science education, careers education, prevocational, business studies and social studies courses.

Resources

If curriculum planners succeed in introducing an economic literacy element into the curriculum for all young people, teachers, some of whom will have no formal economics training, will be faced with the tasks of planning and teaching economic literacy programmes in mixed ability situations. Some resources and materials are now available which incorporate in concrete form, the approach to economic literacy developed here.

The Economics Association's *17 + Working Party*[4] has compiled a collection of teaching resources developed by teachers for use in

other curricular areas and with other target groups of students but
felt to be equally appropriate for courses leading to the CPVE.
Money Management Review[5] Autumn 1983, contains an example of the
application of this approach to the topic of savings. Banking
Information Service material, developed in conjunction with the
Economics Education 14–16 Project[6], and the British Insurance
Association's *Take Cover*[7] pack also incorporate this definition of
economic literacy.

In the autumn of 1985 the BBC broadcast a series of programmes
presenting case studies in production. Together with the ac-
companying teachers' notes and student materials they form a set of
six units each of which is designed to promote the development of an
economics perspective. In one unit, for example, students are asked
to conduct an economics investigation of a slate company and to
develop and apply the necessary skill and concepts. In another unit,
students use the procedural framework to examine a computer
firm's location decision.

The most significant contribution in this context, however, is the
work of the second phase of the *Economics Education 14–16 Project*
which is now based at Manchester University. The report of the first
phase of the project (Holley and Skelton, 1980) described the results
of a survey of the position of economics education in the school
curriculum at 14–16. It showed that relatively few students in the
pre-sixteen age group experienced any economics education. It
identified three groups for whom the economics education provision
was particularly unsatisfactory and recommended that:

> Particular attention should be paid to the needs of pupils for whom
> current provision is least satisfactory, viz: (a) girls; (b) pupils of average
> and below average ability; (c) pupils leaving school at 16.

During the second phase of the project, the members of the project
team, and of teacher groups who have been developing a set of
exemplar materials, have interpreted this directive in a broad way.
Each unit of work contains stimulus material which is within reach
of pupils of all ability, while extension work suggestions cover a
greater breadth and depth of content. For example, the unit entitled
Consumers uses the two contrasting photographs shown above as
stimulus material to stimulate students to discuss the meaning of
wants, and the connection between the satisfaction of these wants,
the level of purchasing power and state provision of goods and
services. Extension work suggestions examine the interdependence
of wants and the differences between necessities and luxuries in
different economic systems.

The units illustrate a wide range of different teaching methods. For example, *Prices*, *Price of a Perm* and *The Ice Cream Factory* use case study material; *Production Record Sheet*, *Journey to Work*, *Tiny Atom Radio*, *Community Expenditure* and *Land Use Planning in the Local Community* contain role-play exercises; *Alternatives*, *Lamb* and *Andy's Car* demonstrate that slides may be used imaginatively in different contexts; *Journey to Work* and *What is Work?* use videos; *The Rate for the Job* includes a simulation exercise; *Accident*, *Vandalism*, *Costs and Benefits*, *Wanting*, *Wages*, *Rate for the Job*, *Two Workers* and *Moving About* employ various kinds of visual stimulus material; *Price of Pop* and *Tiny Atom Radio* include surveys; *Lamb* describes a field visit, *Public Spending* and *Local Authority Rates* are based on textbook material.

Some of the materials require students to reflect on their own experiences of the economic system and to challenge their own personal reactions and opinions. For example, unit A in the consumer module contains, in the extension work section, a suggestion that:

> pupils could be allocated a sum of money and asked to choose the first ten things they would buy with the money as well as giving reasons for their choices. Groups of pupils could be allocated different amounts of money to see whether the choices are very different.

Questions 8 and 9 in unit B of the consumer module require pupils to fill in boxes labelled 'My Wants' and to answer the question 'Will your wants ever be satisfied? Explain your answer'. The consumer module's unit C is based on a survey of shoppers' personal opinions. Unit G is based on a survey of pupil income and spending during one week. Unit C in the producer module is a study of pupils' behaviour as producers in a classroom simulation. Unit D of the producer module contains a suggestion for extension work.

> By selecting pupil responses to the two photographs which relate to the nature of the work being done, the teacher might be asked to open up the area of career choice. Pupils might be asked to choose phrases used to describe the two photographs which might apply to the sort of job that they would hope to do after leaving school. These phrases could be added to by each pupil to get a general picture of what they want in a job. They might then be asked to match up a set of such phrases with a list of jobs given by the teacher. The exact nature of the economics that would come out of this would depend on the responses, but could include job satisfaction, scale of production, wage rates, etc.

Unit A in the citizen module suggests as part of its extension work that pupils should adopt various roles in order to describe the reactions of various people to an accident. Citizen module unit D invites pupils to decide whether or not they agree with one or other of the following statements of pricing policy when applied to categories of goods like the armed forces, holidays, police services, chewing gum, etc.

Statement A – People should always have to pay the full price to get it or use it.

Statement B – People should always be able to get it or use at a reduced price.

Statement C – People should always be able to get it or use it free of charge.

Other units place students in contexts with which they may not be familiar. Examples include consumer module unit D on prices, unit F on budgeting; producer module unit A on prices and costs, unit B on production, unit E on interdependence, unit F on specialisation and mechanisation; citizen module unit B on vandalism. In all cases the units provide opportunities for students to analyse situations which involve a choice in the use of scarce resources by using the procedural framework and thereby to extend their repertoire of skills and knowledge.

The units also perform another function. They are not prescriptive; instead they are intended as patterns and so they contain a range of suggestions for the use of stimulus material. They are thus particularly useful for teachers who wish to adapt the resources and materials to the needs of their own group, and for those who wish to apply the same framework in other circumstances.

NOTES

1 See, for example, the programme contained in the Industrial, Social and Economic Studies section of the Common Core presented in Appendix B of *The Certificate of Pre-Vocational Education-Consultative Document* published in May 1984 by the Joint Board for Pre-Vocational Education

2 Examples which are intended to illustrate this procedural framework are to be found in *Economics in the General Curriculum 14–18* by Steve Hodkinson and Linda Thomas, published by the University of London Institute of Education.

3 This set of procedures is powerful not only because it is an evaluatory framework but also because it helps teachers and students to identify relevant information and concepts. For example, stages one, three and six require an information, skill and conceptual input and it is necessary to allow students to investigate the cost of cigarettes, indirect taxation, factors affecting health, the concept of health as a stock, the tobacco industry, etc.

4 *The Working Party Report on the 17+* is available from the Economics Association, Temple Lodge, South Street, Ditchling, Sussex BN6 8UQ.

5 Money Management Review is available from Schools Liaison Officer, LOA/ASLO Information Centre, Buckingham House, 62/63 Queens Street, London EC4 1AD.

6 Available from Banking Information Service, 10 Lombard Street, London EC3V 9AT.

7 Available from British Insurance Association, Aldermary House, Queen Street, London EC4N 1TU.

4 The Communication System

Ronald Arnold

Introduction

Ronald Arnold has very sensibly concentrated on English language as the major issue in transmitting the communication system by means of a reformed curriculum. The English language is undoubtedly the major means, and schools already devote a good deal of time and effort to this aspect of 'communicative competence'.

But looked at from a cultural analysis point of view there are other aspects of communication and culture that teachers (and not necessarily only English teachers) should be concerned with. Some schools, for example, already offer media studies as a subject to all or some pupils. It may or may not be taught by English teachers. This is one attempt to cope with those aspects of a communication system not covered by a conventional English syllabus. The case has frequently been made for at least two aspects of contemporary culture to be included in the curriculum in some way. First, the non-linguistic symbols which play such an important part in every day life; second, to take account of film and television as important media of communication in their own right – just as important as the novel or the theatre. (Film and television as art forms would, of course, be considered as part of the aesthetic system as well.) Both would involve some elementary treatment of semiology (without, of course, necessarily using that particular technical term). But the aspects of semiology which might be considered to be important for all young people to get to grips with would include signs and signals, gestures and advertisements, not simply as isolated pieces of behaviour, but as part of a society's communication system.

The British Film Institute (BFI) and others have for many years argued the case for including the study of film as part of the curriculum: see, for example, the 1981 Report on Media Education

Conference (available from BFI Education). The influence of television on young people was, once again, discussed in the DES Report (1983b) *Popular Television and Schoolchildren* and commented on in *Television and Schooling* (Lusted and Drummond, 1985). In the past many English teachers have undertaken aspects of work in film, television and other media studies, but ideally every secondary school ought to have a semi-specialist on the staff to incorporate this work as part of the study of the communication system. 'Conversion courses' are now available, such as the MA in Film and Television Studies in Education at the University of London Institute of Education.

Denis Lawton

When we set out to discuss communication as one of the cultural systems with which education is fundamentally concerned, we must at once define and qualify. It is a vast and complex subject. Communication between human beings takes many forms. Language, mathematics, music, dance, and the visual and plastic arts are all processes by which meaning can be conveyed from one individual to another. But they are much more than that. They are processes by which human beings discover themselves, add to the store of their own resources, and make sense of the world. In the study of any one of these forms we must recognise that communication, though a major function, is not its sole function. This is particularly true of the phenomenon of language, to which this paper will be confined. If communication in this mode is to mean anything as one of the major goals of a school, it must be concerned with the whole business of how a pupil learns, and assimilates what he has learned, as well as how he communicates with others.

Language across the Curriculum

This has long been the argument behind the idea of language across the curriculum, a concept which presents the school as a communicative network. The phrase 'language across the curriculum' has by now established itself in the repertoire of educational terms. It first came into use as long ago as the late 1960s, and one of its earliest appearances was in the title of a discussion document produced by the London Association for the Teaching of English, *Language policy across the curriculum* (1969). The theme was taken up by the National Association for the Teaching of English in its 1971 annual conference and by HMI in a series of short courses beginning in 1972. It was amplified by the work of such people as Harold Rosen, James Britton, and Douglas Barnes (1969, 1971) and it influenced the thinking of the Bullock Committee. The Committee's report, *A Language for Life,* argued for two related aspects of the notion: a more active role for the pupil in the use of language throughout the curriculum, and a better understanding by all teachers of the influence of language upon learning. The essence of the first is that the development of the ability to use language has to be advanced across a broad front. Communicative competence cannot be acquired in narrow and limited contexts and then be expected to transfer automatically and with ease to a wide variety of other contexts, some of them of considerable complexity. The school can bring about this competence only by a planned and collaborative effort, with all the staff playing their part. The thesis of the second aspect is that every teacher – and in particular every secondary teacher – needs to know in what ways the quality of the pupils' learning is affected by interaction in the classroom, varieties of writing, and reading demands, and by the experience of these in other subjects and areas of school life. Only in this way will teaching and learning expand out of the transmissional mode which so widely characterises it, notably in the secondary school.

In the years following the publication of the Bullock Report both aspects of language across the curriculum were promoted with great conviction by many LEA advisers, teacher training institutions, individual teachers, and a number of schools. Two substantial enquiries produced further information about the operations of language within the secondary school. The research project based on the University of Nottingham, the findings of which are embodied in *The Effective Use of Reading* by Lunzer and Gardner (1979), showed how much time pupils spent in passive listening and how few were their opportunities for playing an active role in dialogue, or for sustained reading. HMI reached similar conclusions in their national secondary survey, which issued in *Aspects of Secondary Education* (1979). They described the work they had seen as largely teacher-controlled, with an emphasis on the instilling of facts at the expense of exploring the ideas and concepts behind them. In the 380 schools that formed the sample they saw very many lessons where the pupils were restricted to brief responses to teachers' questions, with little opportunity to exchange ideas or examine hypotheses. If talk was scanty, writing was copious, and it was not unusual for pupils to produce nearly a quarter of a million words across, say, six subjects in a two year course running up to a 16+ examination. Much of this writing was confined to the restatement of facts, with few opportunities for the pupils to develop it for a variety of purposes. The language chapter of this report argued a strong case for all teachers in the secondary school to be alive to the effect upon learning of the kind of language experience through which it was acquired.

With all this powerful advocacy, stretching back across many years, why has there been so little real change, particularly in secondary schools? There have been many courageous initiatives, and even more good intentions, but in most schools the relationship of language and learning appears to be much the same as it was at the time of the national secondary survey. Whatever has been achieved by individual teachers, or by subject departments, schools as institutions rarely consider the operations of language in all areas of the curriculum, and the effect upon the learning of pupils across the whole spectrum of the school's activities. The reasons for this are complex, and it was always unrealistic to believe that simply to devise and adopt something called a language across the curriculum policy would change everything. It was even more unrealistic to expect – as some schools did – that this had to be done by the head of the English department, and to believe that teachers of all other subjects would follow his or her precepts. The specialist teacher of any subject, at whatever level he operates, is always at risk of confining his vision within its boundaries. When this happens there is a loss to the subject and to the curriculum at large.

There are two aspects of this question of the relationship between the constituent parts and the whole. The first is the capacity of the teacher to see his subject as part of the curriculum as a whole and as contributing to it. The second is the explicit making of links between subjects in such a way that the skills and ways of thinking that characterise one are given opportunity for development in others. This attitude of openness has to exist before a language across the curriculum policy can be successfully operated. The only way to ensure that it takes effect is for individual teachers to become convinced that changes of attitude and practice need to be made. They have to be ready to look at the pupil as 'total learner' and 'total language-user'. This in turn means looking to see what is being asked of the pupil in other subjects of the curriculum, and whether the aggregated experience is advancing his learning and his own capacity to use language. It is not the function of the English department to bring all this about unaided, though it will certainly be the department's role to act as a reference point and source of guidance on all matters concerning language.

In short, every school should have a rationale for language, knowing what it seeks to develop in its pupils, how this can best be achieved, and how the success of it can be assessed. Behind this corporate activity must lie a confident understanding of what language is and how it works. To consider how this can be brought about we need to look first at the child's experience of language in the primary school, since it is here where the 'continuity and community of endeavour' has to begin.

The separation of language from the rest of the curriculum is often well established before secondary school life begins. There is a good deal of evidence to suggest that primary schools give a much higher priority to language and mathematical skills than to other areas of the curriculum. The most obvious and the most telling source for this conclusion was *Primary Education in England* (DES, 1978), with the subsequent Scottish parallel *Learning and Teaching in P4 and P7* (SED, 1980). Similar findings emerged from the Oracle project, in *Inside the Primary Classroom* (1980), which estimated a two-thirds emphasis on language and mathematical skills. Other studies, such as the Schools Council *Aims of Primary Education* project (1975) have suggested that schools give a low priority to the development of concepts and skills in what has been called the 'middle ground' of the curriculum, i.e. science, the arts, and environmental studies.

What is more to the point here is that the language and mathematical work is commonly unrelated to the rest of the curriculum, neither resourcing it nor drawing upon it for its prime material.whenever this happens there is at once a danger that language will lose the unity for which the Bullock Report argued: 'A child learns language primarily by using the four modes of talking, listening, writing, and reading in close relationship with one another.' Where these activities are seen as separate skills, to be taught discretely, their development as instruments of learning is impaired.

Reading is a case in point. The three HMI surveys of primary education – published as *Primary Education England* (1980), *Education 5 to 9* (1982a), and *9–13 Middle Schools* (1983a) – all attest to the fact that schools achieve considerable success in the initial teaching of reading. Most schools do not, however, give any concerted attention to developing the skills of reading beyond this basic capacity.

Writing is another activity which is commonly found to be limited in range. In many schools it takes the form only of 'creative writing', which sometimes appears even on the timetable as such, with the other language activities separately timetabled as 'English'. One of these activities might be worth considering in more detail at this point, since it bears closely upon the argument.

The working of 'grammar' and vocabulary exercises is still a widespread practice, despite the volume of evidence which has cast very serious doubt upon them as a means to improving language use. Rice made the point as early as 1903, and the research evidence has since accumulated, that the working of exercises as a discrete practice is a particularly unproductive form of activity in the development of a child's ability to write and talk. The Bullock Report made the point in these words: The child's development of writing ability:

> can be expressed in terms of increasing differentiation. He learns to carry his use of English into a much broader range of social situations, to differing kinds of audience. The purposes to which he puts language

grow more complex, so that he moves from a narrative level of organising experience to one where he is capable of sustained generalisation. Considered in these terms the handling of language is a complex ability, and one that will not be developed simply by working through a series of text-book exercises.

The development of this 'complex ability' in the primary school will depend upon a combination of attributes in those responsible: an understanding of language and how it operates; the capacity to assess performance and identify its characteristics; and the ability to devise a range of methods to make practical advances from that assessment. These methods should be expressions of two basic features: the response to language and the generation of language.

Discussing Language

Pupils should become accustomed, throughout the primary school, to talking about the effects language is achieving in a variety of its forms. For this they will need a metalanguage, and as time goes by they should acquire a body of knowledge which meets their needs. This is a very different business from learning terms through exercises, which – to take an illustration – has been the fate of the parts of speech for generations. Pupils can still be found in primary schools completing exercises which define the parts of speech ('underline the adjectives in the following passage. . . etc.') and pupils can be found completing the same kind of exercises three years later in the secondary school. A pointer to how much this is likely to achieve was given as long ago as 1947 by W. J. Macauley, who found, from a sample of a thousand children, that, after being taught the parts of speech by such means over a six year period, only 36.6 % could identify a noun, 20.6 % a verb, 16 % a pronoun, 5.3 % an adjective, and 3.8 % an adverb. As Macauley remarked, 'Surely some better use could have been made of all that valuable time'.

What is needed is a climate where language and its effects are under discussion at every opportunity. The active discussion of language at work can start early in the primary school and should be an established way of working throughout the secondary school. The whole curriculum should be made a source for this kind of activity, but it will have a particular significance in that part of the curriculum designated as English. Children can be shown, for example, that in good writing there is a curious kind of alchemy at work which endows a word with overtones according to the company it keeps. Words take on connotations from the way they are placed within contexts, and they radiate influences upon other words. When pupils study the writing of language in such ways their command of the metalanguage grows naturally. Discussion of this kind, as a normal part of classroom activity, leaves no participant in doubt about what an adjective is and does; there is a *need* to know, and there will, therefore, be knowing. Measured against lively productive dialogue about how language works in action, the writing of exercises upon words out of their natural context is sterile and futile.

The same creative techniques can be made to apply to the production of language, as well as to the response to it. Children should not write in isolation, their sole audience the teacher as tester. They should learn to work collectively on language, discussing the varying of effects in their own work with the same confidence as that with which they have become used to discussing the work of others. The teacher's assessment will aim to produce a body of knowledge about each child's actual and potential performance in which decisions can be made on where he or she needs to be taken next. It will be for the teacher to decide whether a particular child or group of children is at the right point for, say, some attention to be given to particular lexical or syntactical features. These should not then be taught *in vacuo* but should emerge at the teacher's prompting during the natural and accustomed process of discussing language at work; they would, in short, answer to the needs of audience and function. Thus, the teacher's role would be to build up a repertoire of understanding about language at the same time as stimulating kinds of writing which will create a need for their use. The process is reciprocal, and it calls upon all 'the four modes of talking, listening, writing, and reading in close relationship with one another'.

The Primary School

In this regard the primary teacher is presented simultaneously with unique opportunities and peculiar demands. The opportunities arise from the fact that most primary teachers are still responsible for the work of their class across the whole, or at any rate the greater part, of the curriculum. The demands are upon their professional knowledge and skill in being able to assess language performance and plan the means of improving it. There are two aspects of this set of demands: the state of the art and the extent to which we can expect every teacher to have a command of it.

A good deal is known by now of the early acquisition of language in children. Among the most recent, the work of Wells (1978, 1979 and in Olsen, 1981) in particular has added to our knowledge about family influences upon growth in oral language, and their effect upon the child's transition to the language demands of the school. Kroll and Vann (1981) and Kress (1983) have shown that when children are learning to write they have to acquire different patterns of linguistic organisation from those familiar to them in speech. The body of knowledge that has been built up about language acquisition, the relationship between speech and writing, and the child's early experiences of the written form is of considerable practical value to teachers of young children.

There is less certainty and common agreement about stages of progress in the later primary and early secondary years, and about the best means of assessing it. There have, however, been many research studies and attempts to categorise performance, and currently the work of the Language Monitoring Team of the Assessment of Performance Unit (1981b) is providing valuable data. There is certainly enough material to give the teacher useful guidance in knowing when and to what purpose to shape language experiences to stretch the pupil's capacity.

The question then arises as to how far it is reasonable to expect all teachers in the primary school to have knowledge and expertise of this kind. The answer can only be that if every teacher is to put into effective practice the principles of language across the curriculum, then it is not only reasonable but necessary. Where schools possess a member of staff with special responsibility for language, that teacher will need a deeper level of knowledge, and an understanding of how to make this available to his or her colleagues in achieving these ends.

The Secondary School

Ideally, the secondary school should receive pupils accustomed to working with language in a variety of contexts and in response to the demands of a variety of aspects of the curriculum. We have seen that the organisational structure of the secondary school raises particular problems. The most notable is that there is no overarching knowledge of the pupil's performance as a language user across a wide range of subjects. Generally, there is no means of studying, for example, a pupil's writing performance across several subjects, the kind of tasks he is being set, or for that matter the sheer volume of what is being required of him. Nor is there a means of looking at the range of reading demands being made upon the pupil, the levels of density of the texts, and the purposes to which reading is being put. Above all, there is generally no means of knowing how much chance a pupil has to talk, as distinct from listen, in the course of a school day. Yet this knowledge is critically important if teaching and learning are to be at their most productive. We need to know whether the pupils' experience of language throughout a number of subjects is developing certain linguistic competencies or restricting them. We need to know whether the language transactions through which learning is being acquired are so narrow, so unvaried from one subject to another, that the learning is inefficient. Before looking at how this might be achieved at the level of policy it will be useful to consider in turn the experience of the pupil as talker/listener, reader and writer.

The Nottingham study and the National Secondary Survey by HMI were mentioned earlier as a source of evidence on the ratio of talk to listening in the secondary school. There have also been studies of the *kind* of dialogue the pupils experience, and there is by now a rich literature on interaction in the classroom. Sinclair and Coulthard (1975), Stubbs (1983), Barnes (1971), and Sutton (1981), have all been active in this field – in some cases analysing the nature of the exchange, in others proposing means by which schools can encourage 'talking to learn'.

What is taking place in so much classroom dialogue is the process of initiation-response-feedback, where the teacher defines the area of learning by a tight control of the questions and the nature and shape of the answers that can be offered to them. The pupils are engaged in what has been called 'an elaborate series of endeavours to guess what the teacher has in mind', with otherwise useful responses being deflected because they are not the one the teacher is looking for. It is not the point of the argument here to suggest that the question-answer process is one to be discouraged. This kind of technique has a long tradition and will always remain part of the teacher's repertoire. The argument is that it predominates as a teaching technique, and that the pupil moves from one subject to another throughout the day, spending a good deal of his time learning principally by this means.

Three things are needed to effect change. The first is an explicit understanding by the individual teacher of the limitations of the technique when it steers the pupils' answers and deflects responses which could be exploited. The second is for a common awareness that interaction of this kind is a dominant feature of the pupils' daily experience. The third may well be a collective decision to change practice, ensuring that pupils have opportunities for small group discussion and other forms of exchange which will make 'talking to learn' a reality.

One of the findings of the Nottingham study was that pupils in secondary schools spend on average about 14% of their time in reading activity. Another was that as a general rule this activity occupies short bursts of no more than a few seconds before the pupils are required to do something else, such as write the answer to a question. In other words, the pupil rarely has a sustained encounter with a text, and his brief encounters call for responses which do not allow him to develop a 'dialogue' with it. Goethe once remarked: 'The good people do not know how long it takes to [learn to] read. I have been at it all my life, and I cannot yet say I have reached the goal'. The act of reading is essentially one of uncertainty reduction, the reader using as little of the printed information as he can to get to the meaning. A skilled reader, it has been suggested, constructs meaning rather as the archaeologist constructs the past – from fragmentary evidence and a good deal of general knowledge. Prediction plays an important part in the process, the reader hypothesising possible meanings, confirming and adjusting expectations continually. To achieve this he makes constant use of all the syntactical, lexical, and semantic cues available; in effect, he becomes an active interrogator of the text. These are abilities which the pupils should be helped to acquire, for the process of learning to read is a continuing one.

The first essential is for a great deal more sustained reading than is normally to be found in schools. The range should be wide and the reading should always be for a purpose, not for the completion of some comprehension exercise. As Valéry remarked, 'One only reads well that which one reads with a genuinely personal purpose'. This kind of reading should be found throughout the curriculum, and in every subject there should be opportunities for reading to solve problems, reading to acquire information, and reading for the sheer pleasure of it.

If the pupil is to advance his reading skills across a broad front there are again implications for a common awareness on the part of the staff. One among many matters to be discussed will be levels of difficulty. Some textbooks (and work sheets) in common use in schools have a density of text which taxes all but the ablest readers in the age group for which they are intended. This is not simply a matter of technical words, but of syntactical complexity. Writers of textbooks, concerned to push through a great deal of information in a relatively short space, tend to produce sentences of dense construction, with much embedding of clauses, each encapsulating some new fact. The average sentence length of non fiction is much longer than that of fiction, and the two kinds of writing differ in another important particular. As a work of fiction unfolds, the reader is provided with platforms of expectation. He can predict how the narrative will develop, how a particular character will react, and so on. In one sense, then, a work of fiction becomes progressively easier to read the further one goes into it. The non fiction writer, on the other hand, is continually introducing new information and 'technical' data, with much less support from the 'given' or the 'understood' which is so strongly a feature of fiction. This characteristic of the textbook, and the linguistic construction of so much of the material, can create difficulties for the uncertain reader.

Some very useful analysis of textbooks has been carried out by Katharine Perera, of the University of Manchester. She has shown, for example, that some history and geography books written for 13 year olds have sentences in which the noun and the verb are separated by clauses of twelve or fifteen words. We cannot expect subject teachers to be adept at assessing the linguistic difficulties of the textbooks they propose to use, but we can expect them to know that the problem does exist. Certain professional decisions depend upon this knowledge. Should the texts be chosen with these factors in mind? Should the material be tempered to the capacity of the pupil? Is there a case for explicitly teaching pupils how to cope with certain textual difficulties?

This is only one example of a complex of issues that must govern the development of reading in the secondary school. They include the motivation and opportunities for reading, its status as an activity, the range of experiences it should encompass, and the assessment of the pupil's progress. These are matters about which the whole staff will need to be aware and in which to varying degrees they will all be involved.

In addition to extending our knowledge about performance in writing, the surveys conducted by the APU have produced some interesting information about pupils' attitudes to it. For example, at the ages of both 11 and 15 they tend to think of writing as consisting of two main and distinct categories, the writing of fiction and factual writing. To the first they accord status, since it attracts labels like 'creative' and 'imaginative'. The second they regard as utilitarian, concerned only with conveying information and not with style, variation, and effect.

Also interesting is their attitude to what constitutes good

performance in writing. They focus upon handwriting, neatness, spelling, and punctuation, and only a small minority think in terms of ideas, subject matter, style, and purpose. These attitudes will have been shaped over a long period of time, and they derive from the view they have formed of what writing is for. Audience and function in so much writing in school are narrowly prescribed. It is largely addressed to the teacher as tester, and a great deal of it is baldly transmissional – restating for the teacher what has already been given. In the education of a child as a writer it should be possible to take soundings at any point and find evidence of growth along that continuum referred to earlier: 'from a narrative level of organising experience to one where he is capable of sustained generalisation'. There is evidence that in the secondary school – particularly in the years leading up to public examinations –the great bulk of the writing is transmissional, replicated across the curriculum. It is therefore not surprising that pupils see 'factual' writing in these terms, and that it seems often to have no purpose other than the rehearsing of facts they have acquired.

Valéry's remark can be applied as relevantly to writing as to reading. Development in the quality of writing will come about only if it has the opportunity to fulfil a variety of demands, for all of which the purpose is clear. The function of a piece of writing and the audience to which it is addressed determine to a great extent the forms of language which the writer employs. It thus becomes a matter of considerable importance to make sure that the curriculum at large provides a wide range of demands and opportunities.

School Policy

The process by which pupils in a school learn to communicate and to interpret the communications of others is a highly complex one. It is integral with teaching and learning, and it is the means by which pupils' achievement is assessed in several areas of the curriculum. The school clearly needs a policy which takes full account of the scale of the challenge and makes practical suggestions to meet it. But no ideas, however sound, are likely to take effect throughout the school if they are adopted as abstractions and presented as precepts. Those who are being asked to apply them must first become convinced that there is a need for them.

As part of a school's policy for self-evaluation it will surely be important to look at what is happening to the individual learner as he works his way through a programme of largely discrete specialisms. This can be an empirical process, with a group of teachers from across this range carrying out an investigation. They might select a sample of pupils representing different ages and ability levels, and study how the curriculum is coming through to them. They might choose to gather in and analyse the total written output of these pupils over a period of, say, a month. They might investigate the scale and nature of the pupil's reading activities, and the levels of difficulty they encounter in different subjects. They might arrange to observe the pupils in a variety of lessons through two or three days, noting how much time they spend listening and what opportunities they have to engage in productive talk.

It is from practical investigation of this kind that conviction is likely to arise. What is found will provide the evidence for discussion, and from this should emerge a common understanding of the problem, a set of principles, and some guidelines for action. These should constitute the policy, which will have evolved from a study of practice and not from a ready made set of concepts. As such, it will be subject to change and evolution. Communication is a dynamic process, and the means by which the school evaluates its achievements and shapes its aims must itself be dynamic.

5 Science and the Rationality System

Jon Ogborn

Introduction

The fourth of the cultural systems suggested was the rationality system. The dominant form of rationality in England, as in other Western industrialised societies, is scientific rationality. In the chapter that follows, Professor Jon Ogborn has written about the kind of science curriculum that ought to be available to all young people as part of their common culture. This is a most important aspect of curriculum planning for all schools – primary as well as secondary. But curriculum planning at the institutional level should also keep in mind a number of cultural considerations of a very different kind.

The first is that science provides only one kind of explanation, not a total explanation of the whole of human life. There are certain kinds of experiences – aesthetic and spiritual, for example – where scientific processes and explanations have little to offer. The second point is that some commentators on the twentieth century human scene have pointed out that because science seems to 'work' so successfully in some spheres, it has tended to dominate twentieth century Western thinking. This kind of criticism has used the term 'scientistic' rather than 'scientific' to convey the idea of the mistake of trying to stretch scientific procedures and principles beyond their usefulness, and thereby distorting our understanding of reality. Part of the function of a balanced curriculum will therefore be to demonstrate what science can and cannot do. This is not helped by a 'science versus arts' ethos which characterises many schools; planning the whole curriculum should see different subjects, different forms of knowledge, different cultural systems as complementary rather than competitive.

This distorting effect of science – or rather of scientism – is the result not of paying too much attention to science, but of mis-understanding it. That is why Jon Ogborn's contribution is so valuable in the context of this set of papers. He is careful to point out the difference between science and dogmatism and authoritarianism. Jon Ogborn is advocating 'a broader concept of science' in education as a basis for 'science for all'.

Denis Lawton

Science in Secondary Education for All

The problem of what it would mean for the curriculum for all pupils to reflect adequately the scientific dimension of culture, has in one form or another been on the educational agenda for a considerable time. It has not, however, been an area where much real progress has been made or much clarity achieved. In part this has been because 'all' for some time meant essentially 'all the top twenty-five per cent of the ability range', not *all*. It has been confused by a sense that the very meaning of science changes if it is taught to those who will never use it, or not even imagine using it, as science. Nor, in many respects, has it been a question of the highest priority for schools, perhaps because science has been the subject of much active curriculum development, from which it could be hoped that answers would arrive, rather than having urgently to be sought.

The question has, however, now arrived starkly in front of us, for two reasons. First, many are dissatisfied with the common pattern of studying a little science for two or three years from 12 +, followed by a choice of subject, after which science may play an absent or imbalanced part in the curriculum. Second, the move to comprehensive schools has meant that the problem of teaching science to those who (as it is currently done) do not seem to understand or need it, and who make their feelings all too forcibly known, confronts teachers daily in the classroom.

These questions present themselves largely as questions for the school to resolve, not as problems for government, LEAs, or examination boards, and we ought to ask why this is, without accepting at face value the rhetoric, or ideals, of teacher and school autonomy. Taking a long view, we might say that in the middle of this century all Western industrial countries opted for secondary education for all, but that all are still working out the consequences of such commitment.

That is, by the 1930s, a clear notion had developed of secondary education functioning as a means of selecting people for the more highly valued roles in life, giving it a clear and widely understood meaning in the educational system. Science proved especially well adapted to this sorting out function, providing a graded series of stiff hurdles to cross. The decision to provide secondary education for all did not include a consensus about what that ought to mean. In particular, most parents still saw it (and the selective system helped them to do so) as filling its former function of selection for advantages in life. They thus interpreted secondary education for all as meaning that all would have prizes – prizes which the social system could not in fact deliver.

In this sense, secondary schooling made an impossible promise. It was possible to leave matters thus because of the ideology of local or school autonomy, and teachers and schools colluded in the name of professionalism with the notion that they were responsible for the curriculum. The move to comprehensive schools followed the same pattern, with schools accepting the task of defining a common curriculum, and opening themselves to complaint from government or employers that they were not bringing all pupils to the level of achievement that secondary education for all was taken to imply.

Science is particularly tricky to fit into the concept of a common, widely valued secondary curriculum for all. As a profession, it is practised by a small minority. As a social sub-system, it is influential, expensive and continually throwing up political, economic and moral issues, as well as infecting large areas of practical daily life. As an intellectual system, its difficulty has denied it to most. As a source of many of our notions of reality, truth, and utility, it has immense influence.

In consequence, the simple answers make no sense. It is not enough to say that everyone should know enough science to take part in democratic decision-making (though it is still important to say something like this), because actual issues for decision necessarily have technical aspects understood by relatively few – merely because they are by definition new. Nor is it possible to predict more than a short time ahead what aspects of science will need to be understood for as yet unforeseen innovations.

Nor is it enough to say that science education for all is designed to give people an understanding of the daily physical and technical world around them (important as it also is to try saying something like this). Scientific knowledge generally applies only in a rather indirect way to practical problems in the everyday world, nor is science that part of the cultural system which takes on the task of interpreting the practical world. Instead, it goes further back, behind appearances and the need for immediate action, to understanding in a different and in some sense a deeper way. These deep understandings often have practical consequences, but the nature of those consequences is very unpredictable. (It is perhaps electric light which has had the largest single impact on our lives in the last hundred years, almost doubling the time available for work or play; a consequence not readily foreseen by Ampere and Faraday.)

It is not enough, either, to say that everyone should learn enough science to be able later to go on and study it further (though again this has its seed of truth). That which one needs as a basis to understand harder parts of science does not happily turn out to be just what everyone ought to know. Thus the solving of difficult problems in dynamics, which one can at least argue for as an important basis for further progress in physics, is of precious little use for understanding (say) motorway collisions.

All three 'solutions' are ones for which it is tempting to wish the problems away: to say that science education *must* be about decision making, or about daily reality, or a common basis of shared knowledge. There is enough in such positions to make them plausible goals, and we can have sympathy with those who defend them. But I do not think we shall advance far without soberly confronting the evident gap between reality and such aims, and then not blaming the gap solely on deficiencies of teachers, pupils, or of 'the system'. Some of the difficulties are, I believe, inherent in the nature of the subject.

The Curriculum Planning Problem

This discussion is set in a context of curriculum theory, particularly of justifying in some fundamental way the allocation of space, and the content and structure to fill that space, in the curriculum. To argue in this way is a common academic custom, perhaps a favourite pastime. Before playing that game, we ought to ask whether it is the right one to play in the circumstances; whether its questions mesh well with the nature of the problems we face.

Consider for a moment curriculum planning as architecture. Architecture can be done at several levels. There is the level of Le Corbusier, planning whole environments from first principles, inventing new organisations and structures. Much academic discussion of the curriculum falls in this mode, and as with Le Corbusier, the plans are rarely built but the ideas have surprisingly large long term influence.

Then there is the level of town planning, again reshaping whole environments, but now generally within an agreed set of 'obvious' ideas about organisation. There will be cars, or academic subjects, even though a Le Corbusier may undermine their validity as design elements. Such perhaps is the normal level of whole school curriculum planning.

Not at all to be despised is the level of the jobbing builder, putting up houses one at a time without a master plan, meeting an immediate need or exploiting an opportunity. And, just as (if we have eyes to see) much of the best of our built environment arose in just this way, so much that is best in the curriculum arrived by a similar route. In science education, for example, people are currently reshaping the curriculum by building pieces of teaching around electronics and microcomputers. Others are working out ways of teaching science outside the classroom, in industrial or natural settings.

Also influential in architecture is the commercially oriented architect of office blocks, who, to the annoyance of those with higher ideals, meets fierce constraints and still wins customers. Such is the influence on the curriculum of textbook authors and publishers.

Finally, a significant but much ignored architectural problem is that of mending the roof in an emergency. Not a little of school based curriculum work is in this mode, with new courses worked out because of serious and urgent problems with present ones, with the solutions rightly determined by immediate practicalities, including expense and staff available.

It seems that a discussion of problems and solutions concerning science in the common curriculum cannot usefully stay at one level, nor ignore the fact that the various levels exist. A school concerned with mending the roof will have little patience with grand designs; a teacher capturing interest with a new experiment is not dealing with the issues at either level, though what he or she does may contribute to both. Nor is any one level prior, and, in particular, the solving of educational problems is by no means only a matter of getting principles right first and then trying to see how to apply them.

Science and Technology as Social Sub-systems

The standard conception of science education is one of teaching a 'subject', which process leads a few to joining in the activity of doing science. This view tends to ignore a vital aspect of science; that it is a well organised social substructure; generating as a part of the social system demands for resources, for scientists, for education, for recognition; and delivering ideas and techniques, jobs, work and problems. Science is not in books, but in a human organisation (rather oddly organised), which uses books as one device for stabilising its shared knowledge.

It is fairly common to have some such goal for science education as 'understanding what it is to be a scientist'. But the conception generally on offer is only a very small part of the reality, that part to do with knowing a lot, and working alone and as an individual 'finding out' things.

We can draw on John Ziman's writings (1976, 1978, 1980) to expand this picture to something nearer reality as in Figure 1.

In this figure, the standard story appears only at the bottom, where the circle representing individual scientists lies beside and overlaps that representing knowledge. By no accident, the majority of the philosophy of science has discussed just this part of the picture, posing questions about knowledge as questions about how one rational individual could, or could not, accept some single item of knowledge as being the case.

One aspect the standard story touches on a little is that of creativity and individuality, both largely seen as springing from mysterious wells of personality. It says nothing of the social pressure to be novel or daring, to push a technique to its limits, to probe obvious explanations for hidden flaws, that every working scientist is made to feel. Colleagues, critics and referees of papers all work at least as hard as does self-esteem to encourage productive novelty,

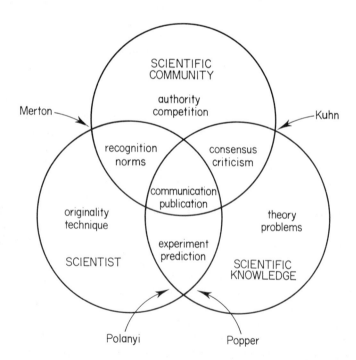

Figure 1   A social model of science (from Ziman, J., *Teaching and Learning about Science and Society*, Cambridge University Press, 1980)

and constrain it moreover to a novelty that seems to be right, not merely novel.

More important still is the role played by the scientific community in recognising work, in effectively enforcing honesty, clarity and respect for the work of others, traits too often presented as meritoriously inborn in those who become scientists. Scientists learn to be good scientists just as mothers learn to be good mothers, even though our culture often feeds us a different story about both.

The scientific community also plays an essential role in sifting potential contributions to knowledge, criticising them with the aim of exposing any flaws, before they are adopted as part of the consensus picture. Nor is this picture a set of patches of knowledge, but is a connected pattern or map, and it is from this that it gains stability, to the point where its 'truth' begins to seem obvious because no thinkable alternative is available. The need to fit knowledge into a whole is the source of what, when science is taught, looks like dogmatism and authoritarianism. We teach parts of science as if there was no other way to think just because, to deal with problems inside that area, there *is* no other way to think for the time being, except the ways we think wrong. This does not mean that the picture is unchangeable, but it does mean that when it changes, it becomes unrecognisable in terms of the old picture, and the old becomes unrecognisable in terms of the new.

All this gives scientific knowledge a very distinctive character. The scientific community is both radically democratic and tightly closed. Scientific knowledge is both extremely tough or shock resistant, and non-conservative. Scientific questions and answers have very little to do with common sense problems or conceptions, though both refer to the same world.

The last point is crucial for science education. Most of us have been struck by how peculiar scientific explanations look; not just against common sense but as somehow belonging to a different world. Of course in time these bizarre notions become absorbed into the common vocabulary, and we all speak of atoms, or of energy, and even of relativity. But it remains the case that science is very much *not* elaborated common sense. Indeed, for an idea to function as an explanation, it often needs to explain the obvious in terms quite unobvious. That my pen rests on the table because the table pushes it upwards is only a minor intellectual oddity to accept; that the passage of time is affected by how fast you travel is much worse. Leaves are green because the chlorophyll molecule is almost but not quite square, ... and so on.

The reasons for this discussion are two-fold. Firstly, we shall not understanding why science presents some of the problems it does when we try to place it in the curriculum unless we understand a little better some of these aspects of its nature, which make it so awkward and refractory, frustrating our simpler hopes or plans for teaching. Secondly, and more importantly, little or no part of these ideas about what science is like even inform the teaching of science, let alone form part of what is taught. Beginnings have been made (SISCON, Science in Society), but there is far to go.

Yet, knowing something of how science works, of how knowledge is built up, and of how scientists work together, is a necessary ingredient of a science education for all. It is here that one may look for a basis for judgements about science, when political or personal decisions arise, not simply in extending technical information to more and more people. What is still lacking are ideas and materials to explain it all in simple terms.

This, however, is not to suggest a conversion of science education into a study of the sociology of science. One good reason for not doing so, and for continuing to see much of science teaching as explaining the current scientific map of the world, is that the existence of this map is what makes the whole enterprise of any importance at all. We need to attach great value to it, and to understand its generation as a social phenomenon is not to relegate it to the level of any collusive group product.

Nor, I believe, is it enough to reduce science teaching to the teaching of scientific processes, as some currently urge. They would identify and give priority to such elements as observation, pattern seeking or problem solving, and some would even deny that the content, which is the vehicle for teaching processes, has any particular importance. Such a view, in terms of Figure 1, makes science teaching inhabit just the small intersection between the areas representing the individual scientist and knowledge, and neglects the rest. Further, such a position is in danger of ignoring the problems thrown up by the fact that some scientific knowledge is more fundamental, more general, more widely applicable and so more important, than others.

Indeed, rather than confine ourselves to one part of Figure 1, I think that we have to set the whole of Figure 1 in a larger picture, as suggested by Figure 2 (adapted from Ziman, 1980).

Figure 2 recognises realities that the pure scheme of Figure 1 ignores. It accepts that modern science depends on large scale and expensive apparatus, funded to large institutions, the management of which pose problems of policy, economics and administration. It

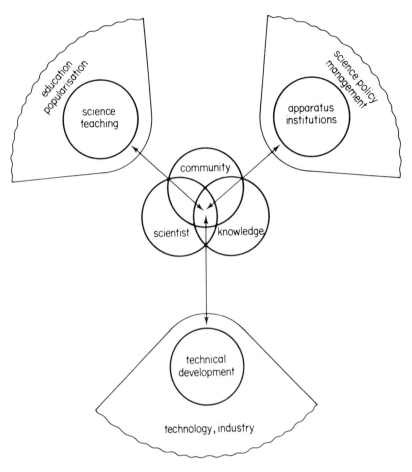

Figure 2 Science within the technical-scientific social structure (from Ziman, J., *ibid*)

accepts that science influences and is influenced by technical developments, themselves part of the technological sub-system of society. Finally, it accepts that science and scientists interact strongly with the rest of society, through the education system, and very importantly, through popularisation of new ideas and techniques.

This last point means that to pose questions about science education, we have to see science education as part of the social structure of science and technology, not as an interface between an independent system of science and the rest.

Checklists for Science Education

A number of checklists of aspects of science, its nature, content, social structure and its relations to technology and to culture are now proposed, which may be a helpful basis for curriculum planning. They could no doubt be extended, but their purpose is to suggest an outline structure within which thinking could develop, not to specify every detail even were that possible.

Checklist for the social model of science

This suggests three main headings under which we can ask whether a science curriculum begins to present an adequate picture of how science itself works. They are obtained by looking at the relations between the three main areas of Figure 1.

Knowledge and community

Are there elements in the curriculum which illustrate how, through criticism aimed at a consensus, reliable scientific knowledge is fabricated? For example, is it shown how ideas such as atoms, evolution, or the interpretation of the fossil record, have passed through phases of dubiety to their present status?

Scientist and Knowledge

Are there examples of how a person's idea or technique deals with (or creates) a problem in current knowledge, and contributes to solving such a problem and generating new ones? One might cite as instances the invention of the microscope, the exploitation of the computer, or the parallel technical and the theoretical development of electricity.

Scientist and Community

Does the curriculum show cases of the interaction of attempts to contribute to knowledge, and recognition of them? Is it shown how scientific behaviour is moulded by such interactions?

Checklist for the character of scientific knowledge

The curriculum ought surely to communicate the rather special character of scientific knowledge. Amongst many aspects that might be selected for attention:

Things are not what they seem

Examples such as atoms, disease-causing microbes, or the nature of stars, can bring out how scientific explanations, because they do really try to be explanations, are often driven back behind the surface of things, creating a new world of entities and whole new levels of description. These in their turn become new objects of investigation.

Belief and Doubt

Science raises very deep questions about belief and doubt, as may be illustrated by such examples as Continental drift, evolution, or Kepler's laws (including those we now ignore). In particular, it raises (in the words of Polanyi, 1958) the need to 'hold firmly to what I believe to be true, even though I know that it might conceivably be false'. Scientific knowledge is both tough and fragile, both as sure a knowledge of its kind as we have and open to change or revision. Nor is this a paradox; the very 'certainty' of scientific explanations derives from the possibility that they can change.

New Knowledge leads to New Problems

Science is not at all like the slow mapping of a finite surface. Rather, new understandings lead both to new kinds of power and to new kinds of problems. Examples can be taken from nuclear power, biotechnology, genetic engineering or drugs. It is clear that, whether we like it or not, scientific and technical knowledge has an in-built growth dynamic which it is foolish to ignore.

Know-how Matters

Much more of science is to be understood in terms of the importance of know-how than is commonly allowed. Sheer technique, not necessarily dazzling, lies behind the construction of nearly all experiments. For this reason, we ought to ask whether the curriculum sufficiently stresses know-how of such kinds as plumbing, soldering, wiring, heating and so on. There is an important pride in craftsmanship which is rarely sufficiently valued in school science.

Checklist for science in context

The science curriculum ought, in my view, to exemplify how the main elements illustrated in Figure 2 work.

Science and Policy

Examples such as the funding of CERN, of cancer research, of a big laboratory, or even a study of bulletins of the Science and Engineering Research Council, might bring out how science is not, in general, done purely by individuals in isolation, but that it involves issues of political decision, judgement, and influence.

Technique and Technology
Technology, too often seen as applications of principles, actually plays a much more dynamic role. Questions could be raised about whether medicine is a technology, about how the technology of electric power generation developed and works, or about the multiple ways in which plastics have influenced our lives and needs.

Popularisation
We need to ask where the curriculum will come to terms with the accounts of science which make it available in other ways. Magazines and television programmes tell of the origin of the Universe or the nature of life, where the traditional science curriculum rather conspicuously does not. Any bookshop will sell you rather high level technical magazines about computers or electronics, which communicate at a level the science curriculum would define as too high, and do so to a substantial number of people with little scientific background.

Checklist for content areas

It is difficult to get away from definitions of content in terms either of subjects or of large theoretical concepts. If we ask which concerns of our culture are importantly addressed by science, we may do better. This leads me to suggest five areas which ought to be represented, in selecting content.

Life
What does science say about the nature of life, and its possible origins? How do we understand life, death, and the interdependence of living things?

The Material World
What do we know about the nature of the matter around us: stones, earth, water, air? How are their properties to be understood?

The Made World
How are materials and structures which work as we want to be devised? Why, for example, are metals and plastics as they are? How, for example, are bridges built? How can homes be heated and kept dry?

Systems
How are such cooperative structures as power systems, computers, or water supplies put together, organised and managed? When are they stable, and when not? How does feedback influence their behaviour?

Know-how
How does one do such useful things as soldering, making a table stable, polishing and shaping, cutting and bending, tilling soil, pruning, or keeping a pond alive?

It ought to be serious worry that such valuable and culturally important skills and forms of knowledge are, in our conception of science teaching and its relation to craft, design and technology, at once problematic.

Conclusion

Perhaps the central problem not faced here is that the view of science education offered involves a widening of the conception of science in education, at a period when constraints on the time science should occupy are stronger rather than weaker. Yet it seems to me that a broader conception of science is essential, because of the wider needs of a science for all, because of the need to offer even a faintly adequate picture of science as it exists in our culture, and because of the increasing importance of a wide variety of issues relating to science and technology.

The nature of the broadening is such, involving as it does the interests of other subjects such as craft, history, economics and sociology, that there will have to be an element of science across the curriculum in any curriculum planning. And to say that is, of course, a way of underlining the difficulty of the problem, not an easy escape from specifying a science curriculum.

6 The Technology System

Tom Dodd

Introduction

In many respects the technology system is the most obvious aspect of any culture; to the anthropologically naive, technological differences are *the* cultural differences. It is, therefore, surprising that so little account has been taken of the relationship between technology and curriculum planning.

Recently, however, it has become fashionable to blame the education system for the failures of industry; it is alleged that for various reasons the curriculum has failed to produce the kind of manpower needed by commerce and industry. Especially since 1976 there has been a tendency to encourage schools to move in the direction of vocational training, and also to switch funds from the DES to various training agencies in order to emphasise technical training. Such trends might be dangerous. The real need is for curriculum planners to take the technological aspects of a culture as central to improving the understanding of our society in the twentieth century as well as producing a better workforce. Teaching low level skills with little transferability will be an expensive and futile alternative to the kind of radical reform of curriculum that is needed.

Tom Dodd's chapter is particularly valuable in explaining the broad approach to technology in the curriculum. He demonstrates the need for technological education rather than technical training. His own wide ranging career has admirably equipped him to discuss this aspect of curriculum change: he was an officer in the Royal Engineers, a teacher, a teacher trainer and a Senior Inspector for Craft, Design and Technology, before joining the Manpower Services Commission.

Denis Lawton

The task in this chapter is to delineate the technological system within the general cultural and curriculum framework, so that later we can begin to examine ways in which it may be handled in schools.

A look at the dictionary will tell us that technical is 'of the mechanical arts and applied science generally', and that technology is 'the art of making things' or 'the application of human and material resources to satisfy human need'.

The latter definition establishes the important relationship between things (products) and people. Designers and technologists constantly explore this interface between people and their needs when they design and manufacture products. Often we say that they have failed to solve the problem adequately, as we can illustrate from our annoyance and discomfort on many occasions. The chair which induces numbness and pain after the lecture has been in progress for half an hour, or the plastic cup which when filled with tea is impossible to hold, are examples of technology. So also is the Rolls Royce car, the Boeing 747 and the Thames Barrier.

The shortcomings of the technologist tend to be noted because of the need to balance a wide variety of design considerations at the planning stage. Politicians, managers and other groups encourage the technologist to compromise according to the needs and beliefs of the individual or group. Safety, cheapness, ease of production, simplicity, looks, etc. are uneasy bedfellows, and the outcome, in terms of the product, will reflect these cultural pressures, priorities and beliefs. The environment we have created illustrates our way of life, our priorities, what we are prepared to pay for, and emphasises our social patterns.

It is interesting to note that in most previous curriculum analyses technology has not appeared, probably because they have usually been based on bodies of knowledge or traditional academic divisions. Technology, however, is an integrating activity which draws on many different disciplines; it has a practical and experiential element; it depends on fusing the qualitative and the quantitative aspects of designing. Thus it does not easily fit into the conventional areas of scholarship. However, it is through this activity that we have fashioned our world and determined much of our quality of life. Payan (1972) illustrates this point when he says: 'Technology is a means of culture – a means of situating oneself in relation to the modern world, in the technical and human aspects which characterise our civilisation'.

Deforge (1972) suggests that 'an educational system which will not accept technology, is an educational system which turns out cultural cripples'. Until quite recently this criticism applied to much of our school system, which offered some craft studies and some science (of a rather pure kind) but largely ignored technology in any significant sense.

The growth of newer programmes of design and technology has begun to fill the gap, but the school curriculum is still largely based on academic disciplines and discrete subject forms. Recently the emphasis which has been given to technical and vocational elements within the curriculum through the government sponsored TVEI has underlined the deficiencies (MSC, 1984).

Comparisons

It may be useful to look at what others regard as technological in curriculum terms. For example, Australia takes a surprisingly similar approach in its courses. The notion of project work through which the pupil is encouraged to design and make a product is central to both systems. What is different is the kind of problem tackled by the pupils in each country. Australian pupils are concerned with conserving water, and the design of guttering, down spouts and collection tanks is a real and immediate problem to them. The same could be said about solar heating and certain kinds of farm equipment.

What is common is that we both believe in using the technological process of designing and manufacture as a learning experience for pupils in school. The activity provides a problem solving opportunity which is both real and attractive. It promotes experiential learning and provides opportunity for using the more formal 'tools of learning', acquired elsewhere in the school curriculum, for the solution of real problems.

Dr Maley (1983) indicated that there was a considerable level of agreement about the nature of technology programmes in Europe. The countries involved in the study were Austria, Cyprus, the Federal Republic of Germany, Greece, Malta, Portugal, Spain and Turkey. From the many points made six are extracted here which are useful in indicating the nature of technology in schools.

1 Technology operates from a practical base and is partly concerned with the acquisition of practical skills;
2 Technology is to do with the creation of an artificial world which reflects the needs and interests of society and the individual;
3 Teaching emphasises planning, organisation and calculation;
4 The teaching style is different from the classical type in

that it focuses on the needs, interests and development of the individual.

5 Technology emphasises the discovery of the outside world and contributes towards values appropriate to that society.

6 Teaching technology emphasises creativity on the part of the pupil.

Process

To understand the emphasis put on the development of technological studies in schools it is necessary to make the distinction between designing as a process used in industry, and designing as a learning activity in schools. The industrial process depends on the efficiency, appropriateness and marketability of the product and the process is adapted to achieve these ends. It can operate at the level of the craft operative or in the more sophisticated areas of high technology.

What we in education have done is to take this process into schools to promote learning of an interdisciplinary kind which emphasises the technological component in our culture and provides first hand experience of real life problem solving. There is a clear change of emphasis because although on the surface the process appears to be the same as that for industry, the real educational benefits are those which accrue to the child from actually participating in technological development. The product remains an important goal which gives meaning to the process. But it ceases to be the only one, or even the main one. The educational goal is a change in the pupil, rather than what is produced by the pupil, although 'the product' may be used as part of the evaluation of the process.

In technological project work the pupil is asked to assume the roles of customer, designer, draughtsman, manufacturer and evaluator, and it is the totality of this package which helps the pupil to make sense of the many abstract concepts. Technology requires the pupil to develop (at an appropriate level) skills of discrimination, decision making, analysis, synthesis and evaluation. The pupil is required to weigh up the evidence, make important value judgements and, often, to compromise.

This process of technology provides important feedback about success and failure, and the pupil is constantly involved in assessing his progress. The Engineering Industry Training Board produced a useful report *The Relevance of School Learning to Performance in Industry* (1977), which underlines the important benefits which accrue from this kind of learning. The report highlights the importance of practical/experiential activities because, amongst other reasons, they enable a pupil to develop important transferable skills, like planning, which are crucial in adult life.

School Subjects

In schools the subject of CDT (Craft, Design and Technology) provides a base for the development of many technological activities. Unfortunately, because most subjects tend to be isolated, the interpretation of technology rests with a small group of teachers. In practice, some teachers emphasise the importance of the product (concentrating on the 'craft'); others place greater stress on the relationship of product to individual, with emphasis on the social and other issues (design). And teachers who emphasise the technological dimension tend to concentrate on the applied science and mathematical knowledge base (technology). This fragmentation is largely the result of the traditional training routes and the unfortunate divisions within the school curriculum at the present time.

Technology should be an integrated activity which fuses these three dimensions into one coherent approach. Take, for example, the design of a hair dryer and the many design considerations which need to be applied. There are both qualitative and quantitative judgements and decisions to be made, and the product reflects the interpretation of matters as far apart as shape, strength, colour, ease of service, cost, efficiency, safety and style.

There are many different activities which occur under the title of technology, but there is a clearly recognisable cognitive process which runs through them all. It is a sequence by which we ask questions in a logical form, and this provides us with a strategy for solving problems of this kind.

Project Work

It is important to look at what happens in technological project work because it is here that the content and process come together. The starting point for the sequence is the brief, which is either provided by the teacher or determined by the pupil. From this point the pupil will search for ideas and solutions which will satisfy the brief, and from the many possible ideas which will be thrown up, only some are refined and taken through to the final product.

Through the planning process rough sketches, calculations, constructional possibilities are transformed into working drawings. Divergent thought patterns become more focused as the process develops. Production and manufacture follow, with inevitable modifications, before the pupil and the teacher begin to assess the final solution against the original design brief. Evaluation is thus an important aspect of the learning cycle.

If it is accepted that project work is a central theme, it will also be apparent that the teacher will need to arrange for a variety of inputs which will enhance the knowledge, skills and abilities of the pupil. Many design skills are acquired elsewhere in the school curriculum, but often it is through the technological project work that the pupil learns how to apply them in a useful and appropriate way.

Initially, the technology teacher provides a supporting structure within which pupils can tackle their project work. The aim will be to encourage them to develop their own strategies and to by-pass the formal structure when they begin to make more self-confident leaps. The essence of technology is its 'design-make-test' routine as witnessed through the many industrially sponsored schemes like the Young Engineer for Britain, Build-a-Car and Schools Design Prize.

By looking at current developments in technology we are directed to a model which perhaps simplifies a system which is concerned with both the content and process of 'making things'. Geoffrey Harrison's model (1981) is based on three functions which are compatible with the picture of developments so far. They are *Resources, Capability* and *Awareness*.

Resources (knowing and knowing how)
- of fundamental and applicable knowledge,
- of physical and intellectual skills,
- of experience.

Capability (doing)
- the ability to dream, imagine and invent,
- to solve problems,
- to create and put dreams into practical effect,
- to gauge effect and significance of action and inaction.

Awareness (knowing about and knowing why)
- self consciousness and social consciousness – awareness of potentials, relationships, implications and obligations;
- appreciation of cultural heritage, traditions, and of aesthetic values, motivation, excitement, sense of purpose.
- understanding of historical development.

If we now begin to put some flesh on that model in terms of the technical/technological dimension we begin to come up with a checklist for those concerned with curriculum planning. Questions arise about strategies which teachers might adopt for ensuring that certain content areas are covered, also about cross curricular policies for dealing with areas like graphicacy and the process of learning.

If we consider some examples of the detail of the Resources dimension it can be seen that many existing school subjects contribute at the moment:

- knowledge of materials and their economics, workshop processes and the techniques of forming and joining materials and components;
- knowledge of structures and mechanics;
- knowledge of power, energy sources and energy transfer systems;
- knowledge of measurement instrumentation;
- knowledge of control systems, etc.

Similarly, in looking at the second dimension of Capability it is clear that such developments are not subject based, but require a wider curriculum treatment:

- the ability to use enterprise, resourcefulness and determination to achieve practical, purposeful and valuable end results;
- the ability to solve real problems at a personal, social or environmental level through the creation of functioning things, devices, systems or organisations;
- the ability to recognise, identify and specify needs capable of being met by a practical solution. The ability to dream up possible solutions and follow them through the processes of selection and optimisation to the detailed design stage, and/or to the precise processes of execution of the creative manufacture and evaluation of the final product, i.e. the capability to get things done.

The third dimension underlines the important broad base required in the attitudes and values appropriate to technological understanding and competence in a rapidly changing society. Without this broad base an aspect of technology becomes *an aspect of* quantitative applied science – attractive in university departments, but lacking in the wider areas of human endeavour.

It may appear that the whole of the curriculum will need to be directed at 'technological development' – perhaps this underlines the relationship with other areas of knowledge:

- the history of the fundamentally creative activities of humanity,
- the culture of the arts and manufacturers,
- the interdependence of the arts and the sciences,
- appreciation of aesthetic values,
- the national and personal economic necessity to create and earn a living,
- the role of technology in meeting the needs of the less fortunate,
- the need for self-drive and motivation,
- the dependence upon appropriately high standards of work for a device to function properly,
- the satisfaction of completing a job well done.

Attitudes develop as a result of personal experience and personal conviction in many different areas of education and life generally. The contribution of the humanities and sciences can be clearly seen as playing a vital role in Technology.

Such a model provides us with a pattern of what Technology might mean within the context pattern of the total curriculum. It hints at the relationship between existing subjects, and questions *our* traditional 'division of labour'. The cross curricular threads are exposed and the need for teachers to devise strategies which will provide links between what are often isolated bodies of knowledge. The traditional curriculum has been delincated largely in terms of knowledge to be acquired. Technology (as a system in this sense) exposes the need for teachers to look much more closely at the process and method of education as well. Unless this is done we will always be designing a curriculum which lines up with the university 'subjects'/disciplines rather than with the need of pupils being educated in a culture like ours.

Supposing that teachers do accept the need to look at the curriculum from a different perspective, through the cultural systems, there are many questions to be answered about the actual management of change. Perhaps a useful first step is to eradicate some of the duplication and discontinuity which exists, expose the overlaps of interest, determine priorities and begin to plan coherent packages of learning. We have to start from where we are and that means incorporating subject centred teachers into these newer strategies.

A developing model for each school, in Technology alone, is a complex 3D form layered into years. It may be difficult to use it in the practical environment of the school but it should, at least, suggest that a more appropriate and rational approach to planning might be considered.

A further task awaits teachers and that is to consider how Technology relates to the content and process of the other systems. What organisational changes will be necessary if we are to increase the relevance and effectiveness of what is learned at school? Technology is central to our culture but a look at current school curricula might not expose that fact.

7 The Morality System

Lionel Ward

Introduction

Whilst it is not very difficult in simple societies to pass on a moral code which is understood and unquestioned by all, in a society where 'morality' is a topic of debate, the moral education of the young is much more difficult. Instead of learning fixed rules, pupils must understand and internalise the more abstract principles underlying those rules. Rules may change from time to time or place to place, but principles are universal. This is not only a difficult lesson to learn, it is much less easy to teach.

Our society in the 1980s is not only a society which has ceased to be one in which morals can be closely related to religious doctrine, it is also a society which is multi-cultural. Even if Britain were still a largely Christian society, the fact that there are so many children in our schools whose background is non-Christian, makes it necessary for us not only to teach moral rules, but also to look beyond those rules to the principles which underlie them.

In the chapter that follows, Dr Ward discusses the whole question of moral development both from a universalistic point of view in keeping with the research of Lawrence Kohlberg, and also from the practical point of view of dealing with moral development and moral education in the classroom in a pluralistic and multi-cultural society.

Denis Lawton

Mediating the moral aspect of culture to children has a long history and is an international concern.[1] Currently, in Britain it has acquired a new sense of urgency. Moral education, by which is meant assisting young people in their moral development, has always in some measure involved conforming those being taught to those standards of right and wrong, both in thought and behaviour, which any society has generally accepted at any stage in its history. Despite claims to the contrary, and although alternatives to this somewhat indoctrinatory kind of moral education have existed, morality in the school curriculum has been taught largely on the basis of a moral consensus.

In recent years this consensus has been increasingly hard for the teacher to gauge. While it will be the purpose of this chapter to suggest that the apparent loss of consensus has been exaggerated, and that the lack of a unitary moral code has had too inhibiting an effect on teachers, it would be foolish to deny that the Reformation, the rise of Science, industrialisation, urbanisation, utilitarian philosophy, the advent of a multi-ethnic society, and the decline of adolescence as a period of apprenticeship and initiation, have all served to remove moral signposts. This has produced what Durkheim called 'anomie' ('normlessness' or not knowing what the rules of society are), and moral relativism (that one system or opinion is as good as another (Lawton in Ward, 1982)). Partly for these reasons, and partly also because of the real or apparent failure in moral education itself as it appears in the behaviour of contemporary youth, moral education has been described as 'arguably the most serious gap in the curriculum in English schools' (Lawton, 1983).

Recent evidence for this wide gap can be seen in the report of the Christian Education Movement, *Religious and Moral Education in Inner City Schools*. The general picture reported of young people's ignorance, teachers' low expectations of their pupils, the enormous gaps between teachers' perceptions of inner city life and the children's own descriptions, the need for more and improved materials which reflect multi-cultural experience and general life experience of children, the need for inner-city experience in teacher training, the importance of in-service training, and the encouragement of formal links between religious education, peace education, political education, health education and moral education, all describe the problem, and to some extent point to broad strategies for dealing with it. These descriptions vindicate further growing concern for that area of the curriculum which had been identified by HMI as the 'ethical' or the sixth in the list of cultural universals or cultural systems described by Lawton (1983).

That teachers have been aware of this serious gap is clear from the survey (May, 1971) undertaken in 1967 in which over 60 per cent of respondents agreed that in maintained schools special periods should be set aside for moral education. Nothing that has happened in society or schools has diminished that need, and an increasing awareness since then of the possibilities for moral education across the curriculum and the powerful influence of the 'hidden curriculum' are a testimony to that growing sense of urgency. About that time R. F. Dearden (1968) was arguing the case for teaching elementary ethics, and he and John White (1973) were attempting to establishing the development of moral autonomy as a major educational objective. They argued that a democratic society involved a form of moral commitment, that in it the young are required not only 'to do the right things', but also to internalise them. That is to say we should encourage our young people to be obedient but questioning, equipped with sets of principles rather than the right answers. How these objectives were to be achieved were then, and still remain, only partly clear. However, May gave some insights into the broad lines along which the subject would be investigated in the last decade and the major aspects of the teaching of morality. There would have to be an awareness in pupils of elementary psychology, an assistance to individuals to develop intellectually, emotionally and morally, an understanding of the formation and changing of attitudes, help in educating the emotions, training in judgement and practice in the exercise of responsibility and self control.

Advocacy of a moral curriculum has always begun with an attempt, at one level or another, to define the nature of morality. Despite the inhibiting effect on teachers of such an activity, for reasons already outlined, the gloomiest view, expressed by Alistair MacIntyre (1968), cannot be allowed to hinder further development. When he expressed the view that moralities vary, just as concepts of morality vary, and that it is still an open question whether we can find a true common subject matter for intellectual inquiry under the rubric 'moral education', he was not being entirely unhelpful. He points realistically here to the difficulties, but offers, perhaps unintentionally, the suggestion that the inquiry may not be entirely intellectual. The concept of moral education offered by R. S. Peters (1961) as an initiation into traditions and into procedures for revising and applying them is not exclusively an intellectual activity. It is this broader view of moral learning that underlies Harold Loukes' comment (Peterson 1965):

the heart of morality is not in abstract moral theory: it is a sense of common kinship, an understanding of the feelings and needs of other people. It begins when we first discover another person, feel him to be real, and recognize that his very existence makes demands on us.

Given this view of moral education, the attempt of Paul Hirst (1973) to establish the existence of morality as one of seven forms of knowledge, important as it is as a precondition for a rational approach to curriculum planning, can be seen as a highly cognitive view and tending to ignore the social functions of education and the capacities of less able children. It is sometimes forgotten that forms of moral learning will take place regardless of the efforts of teacher and school, and the aim of the school has to be to induce in children some measure of conformity to established norms and an internalisation of consistent values within a stable personality. John Wilson (1967) expresses this with a slightly different emphasis: what is needed is an awareness of the feelings of others, accurate knowledge of the facts of the situation, the ability to formulate principles rationally and apply them consistently in one's life.

What these writers appear to be pointing to is the need for the development of the morally autonomous person. Despite difficulties associated with the concept – questions such as the necessity for personal morality, the mistaken notion that moral autonomy must involve moral relativism, and the way in which moral autonomy develops – 'no person can be argued into the moral domain from a position outside; nor can he enter it through submission and obedience to authority' (Wright in Ward, 1982). Tentatively, therefore, we can perhaps describe our task in educating the young person morally in the terms outlined by Derek Wright:

> In referring to the morally autonomous person we mean two things that are intimately connected with each other. He does his own reasoning and makes his own judgments within the domain of moral concepts, the meaning of which he shares with other members of the community of moral persons; and his judgments are associated with a tendency to act in accordance with them, though of course this tendency may not on occasion be strong enough to ensure conformity of behaviour. People are more or less autonomous in relation to morality, but they cannot be moral people without being autonomous in some degree; and the degree of their autonomy can be taken as a measure of the extent to which they are moral people.

The best description of the developmental process by which a person becomes moral is the schema, based on that of Piaget, discussed and elaborated by Lawrence Kohlberg.[2] This scheme has been widely reported, and as will be seen does not give structure to all aspects of the moral development which curriculum planners may desire. However, some understanding of the schema, and how it may be used beneficially in the classroom, is essential if the most influential and reliable insights of research are not to be ignored. In a full description of the impact of classroom discussion upon children's level of moral judgment Blatt and Kohlberg reported encouraging findings.[3]

An outline of the developmental schema through which pupils were encouraged to pass effectively is as follows:

Stage 1   Obedience and punishment orientation. Egocentric deference to superior power, prestige. Avoidance of punishment and acts labelled 'bad'.

Stage 2   Naive instrumental hedonism. Right action is that instrumentally satisfying the self's need and occasionally others. Awareness of relativism of value of each actor's needs and perspective. Naive egalitarianism and orientation to exchange and reciprocity.

Stage 3   Interpersonal concordance or 'good boy' orientation. Orientation to approval and to pleasing and helping others. Conformity to stereotypical images of majority or natural role behaviour, and judgment by intentions.

Stage 4   Authority and social order orientation. Maintaining the given social order for its own sake. Regard for earned expectations of others.

Stage 5   Contractual legalistic orientation. Recognition of an arbitrary element or starting point in rules or expectations for the sake of agreement. Duty defined in terms of contract, general avoidance of violation of the will or rights of others, and majority will and welfare.

Stage 6   Universal ethical principle orientation. Orientation not only to actually ordained social rules but to principles involving appeal to logical universality and consistency. These principles are primarily principles of justice, of reciprocity, and equality of human action, of universal respect for human rights and for human personality.

This study, giving children open dilemmas based on Biblical and non-Biblical material, resulted in the children moving from one stage to another or even skipping a stage, justifying the claim that it was the first research report of a substantial and relatively enduring effect of a formal programme of moral education upon children. It is important, however, to remember that this approach is a matter of cognitive, situational ethics, that there is no guarantee for a similar response in actual moral dilemmas where personal action is called for. Having accepted that limitation, it is worth recording that the American view has been that programmes of values' clarification – where there is a rigorously objective approach to analysing the grounds of moral decisions and an avoidance of indoctrination – are less effective in moral development (Simon, 1972). This may relate to Kohlberg's own admission that within the application of his own schema there is an inevitable element of indoctrination, a fact which many teachers may not entirely regret, given the initiation element in moral education. Teachers keen to evolve a curriculum based on Kohlberg's work will be helped by the workbook produced by Ladenburg and Scharf (1978).

Within this developmental sequence based upon explicit moral education, and pre-supposing considerable theoretical knowledge on the part of the teacher of the schema itself, there are possibilities which have been mapped out most successfully by John Wilson (1969, 1972, 1973a, 1973b). His characteristic approach is to decide logically rather than empirically what constitutes the person 'educated in morality' and to seek the best ways to teach the moral components so isolated. Such components are concerned with key concepts and their sub-divisions as follows: the concept of 'person', the concept of various emotions, knowing the facts, knowing how, practical alertness to moral situations, thinking thoroughly about such situations, making overriding, prescriptive and universalised decisions to act in others' interests, and doing so in practice. Decisions to undertake this explicit approach to curriculum planning in moral education have the benefit of a logically coherent scheme, with suggested approaches, but it is almost inconceivable to see it as other than a form of knowledge in itself. This will not deny the obvious truth that other aspects of the curriculum will be concerned with moral truths, but that this approach is a vigorous explicit form of moral education which can be achieved only by one who has mastered the theoretical framework is beyond question. There will, therefore, in this scheme be lessons in moral education by a skilled practitioner, materials will be constructed to assist the development of the moral components outlined; the Kohlberg schema need not be either ignored nor slavishly adhered to and modes of assessment as outlined by Wilson can be employed.

Little empirical evidence has been reported using Wilson's approach but the work of Simon Bryden–Brook (1972), whose teaching was based on it, suggests that a flexible approach produces valuable results. He comments:

> rather than trying to *train* the pupils in Wilson's skills, one was constructing exercises that would assist the children in identifying themselves with a situation, understanding it, answering factual questions and then in these circumstances starting to make conscious value judgments.

The importance of a supportive school atmosphere is emphasised, as it is by Wilson, and the values of moral education are those of modern education generally, namely logic, open-mindedness, sympathy, order, questioning and responsibility.

It is only fair to report, however, that Wilson's approach has not been without its critics. It often gives the impression of being difficult to implement with the less able and in the ordinary day school. In addition to an almost complete absence of any reference to the cognitive developmental schema of Kohlberg, his approach has been criticised for not going far enough. James Hemming (1980) has argued that moral development is not a tidy linear process, that it involves intuition as well as intellectual grasp, that individual learning has to be supplemented by involvement in social situations, that synthesis is involved as well as analysis, and that complex psychological factors such as modelling and identification are involved.

In marked contrast to the approach of Kohlberg and Wilson is that of the Schools Council Moral Education Project and its Director, Peter McPhail (1972a). It is characteristic of much in moral education that Kohlberg and McPhail agree on what constitutes moral behaviour, but they do not agree on what predicts future behaviour. McPhail's 'consideration' model is based on social learning theory, stressing emotional involvement, habit, rewards, or 'behaviour caught not taught.' The materials produced have been the major input into the curriculum in the moral area. The *Lifeline* material (1972b) had the overall aim of bringing about in young people a considerate life style, and was concerned with how people live their lives, how they see themselves and how they treat others. In the sense that it starts from children's needs it may be regarded as the reverse of the Wilson approach. Set 1, 'In Other People's Shoes' begins with personal intimate situations involving two or three people in the home or neighbourhood. Set 2, 'Proving the Rule' resembles Set 1 but involves more people, concerns group conflict, relations within groups and personal identity. Set 3, 'What Would

You Have Done?' provides actual incidents from the period 1900–
1970, involving racial conflict, discrimination, drug addiction and
vandalism. This material is graded for different ability and age
levels, techniques are varied, the teacher is encouraged to identify
his own position and convey it to the class, and school departments
should decide whether to be involved in what is a 'field of study'
rather than a separate subject. This concept of moral education
across the curriculum is strongly evident in the parallel material,
Startline (1978), for 8 to 13 year olds.

Criticism of the McPhail approach, expressed by R. S. Peters and
others has been directed at its allegedly defective philosophical and
psychological basis. Although there is a detailed description of the
qualities of the considerate adult there appears to be no awareness of
the child learning the moral components necessary to distinguish the
truly moral from the expedient. Inherent in the material (1981) is
the naturalistic fallacy of working from what is to what ought to be.
The large area of consensus in morality makes this criticism less
serious than it might be, but problems remain where there is no
consensus or if the young prefer authoritarian adults. However it is a
five year programme, it provides a framework and there is enough in
it to appeal to supporters of Kohlberg's work.

Finally among the achievements of the Schools Council was the
production of the Humanities Curriculum Project Materials under
the direction of Lawrence Stenhouse (Rudduck, 1976). Their
significance was less in their being assembled with moral education
objectives being central, which they were not, than in their being
centred on contemporary problems from which moral issues are
frequently drawn, the wide variety of materials which may be used
and the controversial notion that the role of the teacher is to be the
'neutral' chairman. Applying this idea the teacher would seek to
select issues and materials in a non-partisan way, use 'neutral'
language, provide learning experience directed towards the acquisition of concepts and skills, and encourage the development of
attitudes without directing precisely what those attitudes should be.
The practical implications of the 'neutral' teacher concept are
discussed by Gerald Gardiner (Ward, 1982) in his review of all the
above approaches.

Throughout all these approaches, however, even that of McPhail
as he readily admits, is the drawback of classroom-based discussion
of hypothetical situations: the difficulty of ensuring a consistent
application of the improved moral insights gained in the classroom
to actual situations. Two articles in the same issue of the Journal of
Moral Education show dramatically opposed views of the relative

contributions of rationality and emotion in moral development (Barley, 1980; Rich, 1980). There is some recognition in all approaches to moral education of the importance of empathy and identification, and there has been a growing acceptance that it has nevertheless been neglected and poorly understood. It is possible that curricula which give prominence to empathetic response, as with the Schools Council materials, will produce a higher correlation between moral thinking and behaviour, but this will have to involve a more profound understanding of the growth of empathy. Stage 1 in empathy sees the person seeking no explanation and ascribing no importance to motives. Other people, whether contemporaries or predecessors, are patronised and viewed as intellectually or morally inferior. By stage 2 motives are routinely assigned to others and there is a recognition that others, contemporaries or predecessors, have capacities for thought and feeling seen as equal to their own. Stage 3 sees attempts to empathise (reciprocate positions) with people in our society or the past. Stage 4 shows a recognition that it is a little easier to empathise with contemporaries than with predecessors, and that there is a need to step outside the contemporary world view. By stage 5 the subject is concerned with the adequacy of empathetic construction, the difference between 'reason for actions' and 'causes of events'. These stages suggest that only at stage 2 is there moral growth, stage 3 represents empathetic functioning and that in our moral situations, despite the relatively objective and vicarious nature of historical material, contemporary issues should precede historical ones. Clearly the associated process of identification has to be understood. Taking the most difficult group for moral education, aggressive boys, a curriculum has to take notice of the evidence of Searle (1972), for example, that such pupils tend to identify with and admire 'powerful' figures in sport, public affairs and the pop culture. Such figures are almost inevitably male, though with girls male identification figures are occasionally chosen.

It has become commonplace to emphasise the role of the hidden curriculum in moral education, though in practice this emphasis has been placed late in the argument. The implication is that curriculum planning will be rendered futile unless all the facets of school life which result in learning which is unintended, or where the intention is disguised from the pupil, are considered and implemented consistently. Consistency is hard to maintain, especially in the large school, but the importance of the hidden curriculum in the drafting of school prospectuses and regulations can be seen in the way in which 'real life' enters into the learning of concepts, skills and

attitudes because they are regularly practised as part of the life of the
school. The hidden curriculum checklist which relates the asking of
questions about the hidden curriculum to the development of the
understanding of moral concepts, encouraging clarity of thought,
developing data or research gathering skills, encouraging creativity,
imagination and openness, a sensitivity to others' feelings and
fostering individual judgment. The authors of this booklet argue
that the whole life of the school must be subjected to the moral
valuing process since education is in itself a moral issue (Cross,
1982).

The logic of this last statement is that even where moral education
is a separate subject, under whatever title, and even with full regard
for the hidden curriculum, moral education will inevitably occur
across the whole curriculum. Birman Nottingham and Michael
Cross (1981) in their paper *Moral Education across the Curriculum*
make it clear that most teachers have an awareness of the role of all
adults, teaching and non-teaching, in a school, that certain staff,
notably the headteacher, RE teachers and pastoral tutors have
particularly important roles, and that all subjects of the curriculum
have significance, though the significance varies considerably from
one subject to another. In its questions to be answered in devising a
curriculum for moral development in the secondary school the
paper highlights the following:

1   Does the school:
1.1   Express in its aims its responsibility for the moral development
       of its pupils?
1.2   Develop a curriculum which:
       – offers concrete opportunities for making decisions and
         acting on them?
       – exposes pupils to situations in which their contribution is
         necessary to the success of the venture or project?
       – fosters their self-image without inflating their egos?
       – minimises the pressure of compulsion?
       – enables pupils to develop independently of their peers
         without losing involvement with their peers?
       – provides for the maximum interaction between pupils and
         teachers as young people and adults?
1.3   Offer library and other resources which reflect the moral
       concerns of teachers, pupils and school subjects?
1.4   Encourage in-service training related to the social and per-
       sonal development of pupils?
1.5   Define clearly the relationship between pastoral care, careers
       guidance health education and moral education?

2 How does each curriculum area relate to the above questions?
2.1 Are their aims related to the moral development of pupils?
2.2 Do the teaching methods used encourage them?
2.3 Does the choice of literature and texts reflect them?
2.4 Do examinations and assessments cover moral issues?

3 What particular contributions can be made by individual subjects?
3.1 Are the pupils given the opportunity to explore the relationship between Art and Society in different cultures?
3.2 How far does the selection of English literature enable pupils to develop moral sensitivity?
3.3 Does the study of English language enable pupils to understand speech and make themselves clearly understood?
   – how far are English language lessons seen as an opportunity to develop sensitivity?
3.4 How far are Foreign Languages used to provide alternative views of important social issues?
   – what sorts of translations are used?
   – do they reflect a particular view (e.g. middle class, sexist)?
3.5 To what extent does Geography underline the importance of global affairs?
   – is the question of how man *ought* to treat his environment considered?
   – are different ways of life in different places presented in bald comparison to local moves or are they seen in relation to their physical setting?
3.6 Does the History syllabus illustrate the perennial issues and values of mankind?
   – is there any study of 'cause'? e.g. are people the authors of their own actions?
   – is the tension between freedom and necessity in human affairs examined? Are the bounds of freedom imposed by situation and circumstance explored?
   – are children made aware of the ingredients of a decision?
   – is any attention given to the notion that choices have consequences?
   – what is made of historical vocabulary like 'Crusade', 'execution', 'Reformation', which are value laden?
   – if ethical dilemmas are presented are they presented solely in terms of a contemporary perspective or are they also set against the situation as it pertained at that time?
   – are motives explored?

- what are the values that are projected in History courses? E.g. is there an assumption that the world, or especially the Western World, is moving inexorably from darkness to enlightenment?

3.7 Is the Mathematics taught related to the needs of individual pupils?
   - to what extent is the assessment of mathematical skill used as a device to re-stream or re-band pupils so that such an assessment has implications for other subject areas and ultimately is part of a much wider social selection?

3.8 How can Music help pupils understand the nature of human emotion?

3.9 Does Physical Education help pupils both compete and cooperate?
   - is social behaviour and sportsmanship discussed, taught, explained, alongside physical skills?
   - what is made of the notion of rules?

3.10 Does the Religious Education syllabus articulate its relationship with a moral education?
   - to what extent are the experiences associated with implicit religion viewed in terms of moral action?

3.11 Does the Science curriculum relate to technology and the future of man?
   - is there any consideration of the role of science in the social, political and decision making process?
   - is there any time spent on investigating division among the scientific community? Or are children presented with a 'consensus theory' of science?
   - is scientific methodology ever examined (e.g. vivisection)?

3.12 In Drama are social situations both within the school itself and within the wider society ever explored?
   - to what extent are children encouraged to explore, express and empathise with different emotions?

3.13 Is the Assembly essentially and intentionally community enhancing or authority enforcing?
   - is there one prevailing ethical base (Christianity) or are a number of viewpoints presented?
   - what is made of achievements within the school?

3.14 Is there a school policy on the use of form periods or tutor time?
   - are form periods regarded primarily as administrative times or do they play a significant part in the social and personal education of the pupils?

In the process of interdepartmental discussions about the contributions of subjects of the curriculum to moral education the suggestion of the same authors (Cross, 1982) concerning the relationship of certain subjects in relation to the development of specific skills may be useful. A matrix describes the contribution of History, Geography, Biology, Religious Education and English to the following nine skills:

1 Classification – development of worthwhile ends
2 Judgment of appropriate means – actions
3 Evaluation of consequences
4 Analysis of intention
5 Evaluation of motives
6 Reasoning skills: general
7 Reasoning skills: consistency, generality
8 Knowledge: information, concepts
9 Making choices.

The necessity of teachers accurately assessing the contribution of their specialist subjects is worth emphasising largely because of the rather facile descriptions that have existed of such contributions. Wilson (1971) has argued convincingly, for example, that religious and moral education are genuine aspects of education, and impinge on the same area of human personality. Jean Holm (in Ward, 1982) has given her analysis of the contribution of RE (in Ward, 1982) and other writers have attempted to assess the contributions of English, History and Science.[4] History and Science are seen as subjects in which there is a strong commitment to a search for factual data, the former providing alternative moral codes, the latter information on which contemporary moral issues, such as abortion, nuclear warfare and euthanasia can be discussed. The potential effectiveness of this approach can be seen in materials such as 'Frontiers of Enquiry' in which issues of childhood, sexual love, personal identity and mental health are considered (Richardson and Chapman, 1971). This approach through subjects, involving some element of team teaching should not be allowed, however, to overshadow the alternative method of moral education where the approach is largely through the form-tutor. This alternative, utilising the fact that the best explicit moral education is conducted in an atmosphere of trust and personal relationship, has been developed with success by Leslie Button (1981, 1974; see also Baldwin and Wells, 1979). The work of Richard Pring (1984) has been partly influenced by the work of Button, and the way in which Pring places the qualities we aim to teach and make explicit in our planning centrally in his approach is a useful complement to that approach which begins with the nature of moral education as a form of knowledge. He lists seven categories:

1 intellectual virtues
2 moral virtues
3 character traits
4 social competencies
5 practical knowledge
6 theoretical knowledge
7 personal values

The matrix he provides for mapping the territory, despite certain reservations which Pring expresses, provides schoolbased curriculum planners with a useful starting point.

	Cognitive Capacity	Facts to be Known	Attitudes Feelings Disposi- tions	Practical Appli- cations
General Considerations				
Being a person (including the capacity for entering into personal relations)				
moral perspective				
ideals (including religions and other sytles of life)				
Specific Application				
Social issues				
– race				
– sexism				
– environment (e.g. political)				
Politics				
– citizenship				
– community participation				
– the law				
Place within society				
– career				
– economic needs				
Health				
– physical				
– mental				

Clearly, as all writers acknowledge, moral education requires in teachers, whether they engage in it explicitly or implicitly, high personal and professional standards, consistency, sensitivity and an exceptional ability in cultural analysis, curriculum planning and practical cooperation with colleagues. Methods will include, in addition to formal teaching, oral discussions, reading appropriate literature, acting, drama, role playing, controlled group therapy, use of films and other media, making a tape, or video tape, games and simulations and making their own rule-based activities (see Wilson, 1973a and 1972). There is no shortage of materials through which the varied aims of moral education, using the methods outlined, can be pursued (particularly: Bull, 1973; Cheston, 1979; Davies, 1972; Dingwall, 1971; Domnitz, 1971; Gardiner, 1984; Martin, 1973; Parrinder, 1973; O. and E. Whitney, 1970; Wright, 1972, 1973.) It is less important that all objectives can be adequately evaluated than the task is undertaken. Asserting the importance of a study of morality is itself an educational objective of the highest importance, and emphasising the importance of moral awareness an inescapable duty of teacher, school and society.

NOTES

1 Historically, 'the appearance of moral education in the school curriculum is reflected in two ways: the changing concept of childhood over time, and views on how mental, physical and moral capacities should be educated; and the challenging notion that social control and order can best be achieved by means of religious instruction.' (P. Gordon and D. Lawton (1978) *Curriculum Change in the Nineteenth and Twentieth Centuries,* Hodder and Stoughton.

   Internationally, moral education can be viewed as a result of the impact in individual countries of the prevailing political, religious and social philosophies; in addition, of course, although there is frequently a gap between what is prescribed for the moral curriculum and what is achieved, another distinction is that between countries which control their curricula and those who do not (L. O. Ward, 'International perspectives on moral education', in L. O. Ward (ed.) (1982) *The Ethical Dimension of the School Curriculum,* Pineridge Press, pp. 26–35.

2 L. Kohlberg (1981) *Essays on Moral Development,* Vol. 1, Harvard University Press. British curriculum planners may accept the claim that the scheme has almost universal cultural validity, including an application in Britain – see A. Simon and L. O. Ward, 'Variables influencing pupils' responses on the Kohlberg schema of moral development', *Journal of Moral Education,* Vol. 2, No. 3, 1973.

3   M. M. Blatt and L. Kohlberg, 'The effects of classroom moral discussion upon children's level of moral judgment', *Journal of Moral Education,* Vol. 4, No. 2, 1975, pp. 129–161. Another study involved older pupils learning about moral discussions, then leading younger ones, and finally themselves developing in Kohlberg's terms – see R. L. Mosher and P. R. Sullivan, 'A Curriculum in Moral Education for Adolescents', *Journal of Moral Education,* Vol. 5, No. 2, 1976, pp. 159–72.

4   Jean Holm, 'The Ethical Contribution of Religious Education', in Ward (ed.) op. cit. pp. 143–165; C. Jones, 'The contribution of history and literature to moral education', *Journal of Moral Education,* Vol. 5, No. 2, 1976, pp. 127–138; C. Jones, 'The contribution of science to moral education', *Journal of Moral Education,* Vol. 5, No. 3, 1976, pp. 249–256; L. O. Ward, 'History – Humanity's teacher?', *Journal of Moral Education,* Vol. 4, No. 2, 1975.

8 The Belief System

Edwin Cox

Introduction

Every society has a belief system. In most societies it is not difficult to describe that belief system. Anthropologists studying simple, pre-literate societies will devote a few pages to a simple description of the beliefs of any society being studied. But anyone trying to describe the belief system of Britain, or any other industrial, secularised, society, would face at least two problems. The first is that there is no single source of beliefs: since the Reformation, Catholic dogma has been challenged; since the Enlightenment, religious beliefs, if not totally rejected, have been limited to only one aspect of life. The second problem is that we live in a society which is not only secular, but is pluralistic. There is no total agreement even about non-religious beliefs, and Britain is now a multicultural society.

The danger is that people – adults or children – may find it difficult to identify their own beliefs, and may even come to the conclusion that they have no beliefs. However, various studies have shown that the majority of the population does share some beliefs, even if they find it difficult to describe them, and even if they are puzzled about them. These beliefs do not come from a single source: they are a mixture of political beliefs (such as the feeling that democracy is superior to totalitarianism; that social justice is worthwhile, that all individuals have certain rights), as well as vaguely scientific or pseudo-scientific beliefs, and some surviving religious beliefs (such as the belief that 'in the end' virtue will be rewarded). These beliefs tend to be shared not only by adults in Britain, irrespective of religious background, but also by the population of western Europe in general. But the difficulties of describing and transmitting the belief system remain. Schools cannot ignore the need to pass on a belief system, but they are often bewildered by the task – understandably so.

Edwin Cox discusses the nature of the kind of beliefs that schools should be concerned with – especially those concerning questions which cannot be answered by empirical statements. He also makes a very important distinction between two different kinds of pluralism, as well as discussing the important relationship between religious education and teaching about beliefs.

Denis Lawton

It has been suggested by Denis Lawton in Chapter 1 that the school curriculum should be structured by reference to certain characteristics which he thinks are common to all cultures. It is the purpose of this paper to look specifically at the belief system and to ask what influence it ought to have on the curriculum, what influence it is in fact having at the present, and what changes ought to be made in existing practice in order that schools may take their appropriate part in transmitting and refining the beliefs which are embedded in a twentieth century pluralist culture, in as far as these are definable.

Preliminary Considerations

Before we can ask what schools are, and ought, to be doing about the fundamental beliefs of society, certain preliminary factors need to be noted.

1   *That the belief system is not independent of other systems*

It may not be closely connected with the communications or technology systems (although both of those presuppose a belief that communications and technology are desirable and beneficial), but Lawton notes that the dominant belief system of any society is closely connected with its morality system. What a society decides is morally permissible is decided by what it believes to be good. Its rationality system is conditioned ultimately by what it postulates about the origins of human thought and the relative importance of diverse aspects of human experience. Its aesthetic judgements, its tastes, are similarly affected by what it assumes to have prior claim on its affections, as is shown, on the one hand, by the joyless austerity of iconoclastic puritanism, and, on the other hand, by the unlimited exuberance of romantic movements.

Beliefs, then, are going to be encountered when dealing with many of the other systems, and are going to have an appreciable effect on the way they are treated. Philip Phenix (1964) has argued that beliefs (what he calls synoptics) are over-arching concepts that are used to combine other forms of meaning into a coherent whole. The effect of this on curriculum is that beliefs cannot be studied in isolation, as an autonomous subject, labelled 'Belief Systems' or 'Religious Education', but will crop up in many parts of the timetable. This raises the question of how the study of them, if it is not to be haphazard and subject to chance, can be coordinated in such a way that teachers will be conscious of what is being taught and pupils will be conscious of what is being learned.

2 *The difficulties of teaching beliefs in a pluralist society*

It is of the essence of a pluralist society that it has a wide variety of beliefs, some of them conflicting. It prides itself on tolerating that variety and conflict and on being able to accommodate any belief, however way-out and idiosyncratic, provided it is not blatantly disruptive of human comfort or obviously and outrageously immoral. Even so, the boundaries of that toleration are so wide and indistinct that they are almost non-existent. It is, consequently, difficult to define the belief system of a pluralist society (apart from saying that it believes in pluralism) or to see how it can influence the curriculum of schools in that society. There may be discernable some residual trends, vestiges of the more homogeneous belief system that preceded the coming of pluralism, and individual groups, such as religious bodies, industrial interests, and sports clubs, may have their own set of beliefs, which they wish to propagate. But any claim that these should be transmitted as definitive is strongly resisted by those who hold rival opinions.

Furthermore, although all beliefs are ultimately tolerated, a pluralist society encourages widespread and open debate about all of them, a debate which is facilitated by the mass media, and consonant with the educational practice of allowing pupils to discover and criticise rather than accept on authority. The result is that, if schools are asked to educate pupils in the beliefs of a pluralist society, teachers may reasonably ask certain questions. Which beliefs? Can we do more than encourage pupils to explore the multiplicity of beliefs extant and to be critical of them? Will such study lead to anything more than relativism and cynicism about all beliefs?

3 *Doubts about all beliefs in a technological society*

Modern European culture is technological as well as pluralist. Technology has been so successful, and has so transformed the quality of life within a couple of generations, that its underlying assumptions have enormous prestige. The chief of those assumptions is that truth is to be found by an impersonal investigation of the behaviour of the material world. Such investigation leads to the discovery of facts which are indisputable, which can be universally demonstrated, and which therefore seem true in a special and guaranteed way. Alongside those proven facts, beliefs, which cannot be so convincingly verified, seem to have an inferior status and are viewed with some caution and even suspicion[1].

This is not to say that a technological society lives by facts alone. Alongside its technological convictions, beliefs abound, beliefs about human goals, about the desirable quality and purpose of life, and in recent years these have become more diverse, and include beliefs about the occult, about the mystic, and about the extra-terrestrial, which previously would have been scorned as outlandish. These way-out beliefs are emotionally held and when pressed or given time for thought most people admit that the proven facts of science are probably superior and definitive. Consequently there is a distinction made between tolerating a kaleidoscope of beliefs and studying them.

The uncertainty of the status of beliefs (as against demonstrable phenomena) produces an aversion to the academic consideration of them, an aversion which can be noticeably strong in secondary school pupils, and which has led to a demand on the part of some educational philosophers that education should confine itself to the 'publicly verifiable'.[2] There is, therefore, a widespread reticence on the part of many teachers to trade in beliefs, apart from those that are so embedded in their own outlook that they do not recognise them as beliefs. It seems safer to stick to the factual.

4 The need to define what is meant by the term 'belief'

The word is widely and loosely used to cover a range of evaluations. There is a diversity of quality in such statements as 'I believe in Tottenham Hotspur', 'I believe in Jesus Christ', 'I believe in being decent to neighbours', 'I believe in rack and pinion steering', and 'I believe in law and order'. Lawton does not make explicit what types of belief he has in mind when he talks of a belief system inherent in cultures which is to be determinative of part of the curriculum. He mentions democracy, patriotism and tolerance as examples, but nowhere advances a definition. It is interesting, moreover, to note how easily talk about 'beliefs which underpin culture' tends to transform itself into talk about values. Lawton, for instance writes that, in spite of the pluralism of English society, 'it is, however, still necessary for schools to work out what beliefs and values are held in common or need to be held in common, and therefore should be transmitted by means of the school curriculum'. He seems to have in mind not superficial beliefs, which are mere expressions of taste or partisan allegiance, but widely held and deeply motivating value systems without which 'society would be in danger of collapse'.

This raises questions not only of what these values are but also of how they are acquired. They seem to spring from answers that individuals give to certain basic questions about reality, such as 'What is ultimately real and abiding?', 'What is the purpose of human consciousness?', 'What manner of life is it wisest (or

happiest, or most self-fulfilling) to seek?', 'What is my responsibility
to other people and to things?', etc. Such questions cannot be
answered by empirical statements, but by beliefs, to which the
individual has to commit himself, or herself, and which consequently influence life styles. They give rise to the values by which
life is lived. When there is consensus in the answers to fundamental
questions there arises a religion or a philosophical system which aims
to clarify and protect the associated beliefs and values.

Pluralist societies come into being when different answers are
forthcoming to questions of ultimate truth and reality. There is a
superficial pluralism when identical answers are produced but
expressed in different images (as when the Christian talks of loving-
kindness and the Hindu of bhakti, or when Islam and Christianity
both postulate a creating theism and one describes it as a
monotheism and the other as a Trinity). There is a deeper pluralism
when conflicting answer to the questions are given (as when one
philosophy maintains that material causality can explain all and
that mental processes are epiphenomenal, and another maintains
that the spiritual is ultimate and material causation merely a means
of expressing it; or when one avers that human beings are temporary
physical mechanisms who are advised to squeeze what pleasure they
can from their temporary functioning, while another insists that life
is lived in an eternal setting and that a human being's ultimate
destiny demands altruism and self-sacrifice).

Our present British pluralism seems to be a mixture of the two.
The presence of the deeper pluralism means that it is very difficult to
decide what are the basic beliefs and subsequent values that
underpin our society and which should be transmitted by means of
the school curriculum. But although we suffer, or enjoy, a diversity
of beliefs and values, they all spring from a common activity of
making decisions about what one is prepared to accept as fundamentally real and sufficiently important to be allowed to influence
one's life style, and it may be in the examining of this process, rather
than in making authoritarian statements about what values are
desirable and to be accepted, that education may have a contribution to make to the understanding of a pluralist society.

Beliefs in the Traditional Curriculum

In the past schools have dealt with beliefs both implicitly and
explicitly. Values of patriotism, toleration, truth-telling, etc. have
tended to be transmitted implicitly, by the hidden curriculum, by

what is approved and disapproved in the discipline system, by stories from history, by traditional tales of heroism, and (more subtly) by discussions of social issues and of situations portrayed in literature. For instance, patriotism was not dealt with by daily flag saluting, American fashion, but by stories of Nelson's signal before Trafalgar and of the boy Cornwall winning the VC. This teaching was unstructured and largely unconscious, reflecting, as it did, the unexamined and tacitly accepted values of the culture. Schools cannot help but teach in this way. Though the values may have changed somewhat, present schools are almost certainly commending implicitly a set of values that are accepted unconsciously and are consequently unexamined. These will have to be brought to the surface and criticised if a structured study of beliefs is to occupy a respectable part of the curriculum.

The explicit treatment of beliefs has been confined almost entirely to the religious education lesson. The White Paper, *Educational Reconstruction* (1943), that preceded the 1944 Education Act saw religious education as the means by which the values that underpinned the culture of the time would be passed on.

> There has been a very general wish, not confined to representatives of the Churches, that religious education should be given a more definite place in the life and work of the schools, springing from the desire to revive the spiritual and personal values in our society and in our national tradition.

This was, of course, dealing with the values and traditions of a homogeneous and pre-pluralist culture. It was assumed that religion (by which was meant Christianity) provided the more or less unquestioned basis of the explanation of existence, of the purpose of human life, and of the requirements of moral action. Therefore an explicit study of Christian doctrines and moral theories would lead to understanding of, and a personal response to, the beliefs and values of Western culture.

It did not work. It might have done if the beliefs of society had been as homogeneous and as Christianly conditioned as was assumed, and had remained so. But the homogeneity rapidly broke down to be replaced by pluralism. This was caused only in part by the arrival in Britain of people from other parts of the world who brought with them other major world religions, Muslims, Hindus, Sikhs, etc. The pluralism was compounded by the fact that many of the native population ceased to profess the traditional Christian doctrines, even when they retained a proportion of the Christian ethic, and now base their values on what have come to be called 'other life stances', which reject a belief in the supernatural and prefer humanist, materialist, Marxist or hedonistic theories. Our pluralism consists, then, not of the presence in our culture of a multiplicity of religions – that is only part of the story – but of a number of religions alongside a number of secular philosophies, and there is the further complication that some people are in the course of transition from a religious view to a secular one, accepting the moral injunctions of a religion while rejecting its doctrinal justification. In a partly religious, partly secular, partly confused pluralism it is not easy to discern dominant values or universal beliefs, much less to teach about them.

Religious education has responded in part to these changes. It has taken account of the more superficial religious pluralism, but been little influenced by the deeper pluralism caused by the spread of secular beliefs. The arrival in classrooms in the late 1960s of Hindu, Muslim and Sikh children raised the question of whether religious education could any longer confine itself to Christianity. Was it to try to Christianise the newcomers, as it had formerly tried to Christianise the indigenous population, or was it to try to help those who belonged to the diverse religions to understand and respect each other? Some teachers chose the former course (and some still do), but the majority widened their teaching content to include the major world faiths. Much published material has been produced on religions other than Christianity and in many schools as much time is spent on studying them as on Christianity. This change was officially recognised in the Birmingham Agreed Syllabus (1975) which allowed secondary school pupils a choice of religions to study. Practically all of the many syllabuses produced since that time have included material from non-Christian religions. Furthermore the purposes of the syllabuses have undergone a change. They no longer aim to convey to pupils any particular set of beliefs, but to present a fair account of the major concepts of each of the religions and to enable pupils to acquire the skills to understand those religions and to sympathise with the attitudes of believers.[3] By these means they hope that students will come into contact with some of the formative beliefs of a pluralist society, be critical but appreciative of them, and as a result work out for themselves what beliefs they are prepared to accept as an adequate interpretation of their own experience.

What Changes are Needed?

The question that now has to be asked is whether a study of religious pluralism is an adequate way of dealing with the explicit teaching about belief, or whether the proper understanding of our culture requires a still wider study which embraces the secular beliefs that are inherent in it. The Birmingham Agreed Syllabus Conference wished to include in their options certain 'life stances' which 'share many of the dimensions of religion while not admitting belief in realities transcending the natural order', but legal advice declared this contrary to the intention of the religious clauses of the 1944 Education Act, and stated that study of such faiths could be undertaken only if it led, by contrast, to a deeper understanding of the religious faiths. The British Humanist Association has advocated including in schools the study of religions as part of a more comprehensive subject called 'Life Stance Education' (1975) (though their recent tendency to abbreviate this into LSE may cause some confusion). Furthermore official publications from the DES have advocated a similar development. *A Framework for the School Curriculum* (1980b) stated that 'it is right. . . for religious education to be linked with the wider consideration of personal and social values', and *The School Curriculum* (1981a) says that 'religious education. . . . forms part of the curriculum's concern with personal and social values, and can help pupils understand the religious and cultural diversity of contemporary society'. There are hints of similar thinking in the preambles of some of the recent Agreed Syllabuses. For instance, Birmingham mentions 'exploring all those elements in human experience which raise questions about life's ultimate meaning and values' and Northamptonshire speaks of 'helping pupils to identify for themselves the fundamental questions of human existence, so that they may continue to reflect upon these and arrive at the decisions life calls for in a responsible way'. It is not clear, however, whether the compilers of those syllabuses envisaged looking for answers to those questions outside religious beliefs.

Teachers of the subject have tended to resist the widening of their work beyond teaching about religions, partly because they feel, perhaps rightly, that their training has not made them competent to deal with the new material required, and partly because they feel that such wider study could not properly be called 'religious education'. But our pluralist culture contains both religious and non-religious belief systems and, if the curriculum is to include a study of beliefs, then some new subject (of which religious education will constitute a respectable part) is needed and an appropriate name will have to be found for it. This is going into uncharted territory, and provokes questions such as 'How do you do it?' and 'What will this subject be like?'.[4]

Outstanding Problems

Before the belief system of our culture can have a consistent influence on the school curriculum, certain other questions need to be answered.

1 How precisely do individuals acquire their values and beliefs? What is the relationship between the two? Very little is known about this and some fundamental research into it seems indicated.
2 What are the basic beliefs and values that schools should advocate and try to transmit?
3 How can those values be reflected in the hidden curriculum and in the attitudes and assumptions on which the various teaching subjects are conducted?
4 Should an attempt be made to teach those values explicitly in specific lessons, which would deal with the religious and the secular life stances by which groups of citizens try to define and express their beliefs?
5 Those who disapprove of pluralism will wish to add a further question. Is it the duty of schools to try and produce a less confused culture by advocating a particular set of beliefs (possibly the Christian ones that formerly pertained) and so restore the 'spiritual and personal values in our national tradition' to which the 1943 White Paper referred?

In a homogeneous culture these questions are superfluous. Such a culture is conscious of its values and of its beliefs from which those values spring. Its whole cast of life is expressing them, and schools do not need to do very much about teaching them, because children are absorbing them from the way their home life is ordered, from remarks of parents and peers, from what is unquestioningly approved and disapproved, and from the way those values are implicitly built into the school experiences. Schools can, however, reinforce this learning by lessons about the belief system that are tacitly accepted by the community, and pupils will have no difficulty in responding to them. No one will feel that something disputatious is being imposed or that the teacher is attempting reprehensible indoctrination.

In a pluralist society the situation is different. No consistent set of beliefs is being imposed upon the young. Curriculum planners may consequently have to choose between two strategies. On the one hand, they may decide that schools can do no more than reflect the variety of extant beliefs and values, telling the pupils of the variety, urging them to criticise the values and to envisage the result of basing practical decisions upon them and to judge whether such outcomes would be welcomed by them. With older students it might be possible to go a stage further and urge them to examine the process by which beliefs and values emerge from ultimate decisions about reality and destiny, as is mentioned in preliminary consideration 4 above. From such studies the pupils will be left to work out their own set of values, even though this might lead to conflicting decisions. On the other hand, curriculum planners may see their task as attempting to bring some coherent view to the young which will guide them through the chaos of pluralism. This would involve a conviction that there are a number of common beliefs underlying our apparent pluralism, which schools should bring to the surface and emphasise. By doing so they would be making a strong contribution to the emergence of a more clearly defined belief and value system than at present pertains and so combat some of the more disruptive elements of pluralism. Lawton may have this in mind when he says, 'It is precisely because there are differences within society between families and other social groups that there needs to be a common system of beliefs worked out which can be transmitted on a consensus basis via the school curriculum'.

The problems connected with trying to include values transmission in the curriculum are considerable. Firstly it is necessary to decide what are the common values. At present we might agree on liberty, freedom, democracy, fairness, and care for the unfortunate; but the emergence in recent years of aggressive self-assertion, admiration for financial and social success at any cost, and the increasing use of 'muscle' to advance partisan causes make one wonder whether liberty, freedom and fairness are still the operative values. Do we know any longer what values schools are to transmit? Secondly who is to make the decisions about which values the curriculum is to reflect? Is it the government of the day, via the DES, Local Education Authorities, teachers' organisations, or is it to be left to individual schools to decide? Do we perhaps need a body to decide what beliefs are agreed, on the lines of the Standing Conferences which draw up Agreed Syllabuses of Religious Instruction? Thirdly, would not any attempt to prescribe what values are to be taught be regarded as unduly authoritarian, as an attempt by a moralising minority to impose their personal convictions on the community? Will liberal educationalists of a truly plural society tolerate using schools to moderate its pluralism? Which leads to the somewhat unsatisfactory conclusion that though a belief system may be a determinative aspect of a culture, and where that belief system is defined and accepted it may be taught in the schools, that situation does not pertain in Britain at present because a single belief system is neither defined nor accepted. As long as there is no concensus about our basic operative beliefs and values, their influence on the curriculum is going to be problematic.

NOTES

1   This judgement of the superiority of demonstrable fact over belief is itself a belief. It is no longer shared by leading scientific and philosophical thinkers, but it fuels much popular thought, especially among seconday school male pupils.
2   See P. H. Hirst 'Morals, Religion and the Maintained Schools' in C. Macy (1969). Hirst's more recent writings suggest that he has modified his position.
3   Recent syllabuses tend to aim at giving knowledge (of religious concepts), skills (to understand) and attitudes (of tolerance and openmindedness).
4   A tentative answer to these questions can be found in Chapter 10 of E. Cox (1983).

9 The Aesthetic System

Ken Robinson

Introduction

Dr Ken Robinson clearly has some doubts about the title proposed for his chapter. He is not sure whether it is appropriate to talk of the arts in terms of an aesthetic *system* – any system might be considered to be too restrictive to cope with the essentially unpredictable nature of creative activities. I would agree completely if the word 'system' were being used in the restrictive sense of 'systems theory' with its clear boundaries, unambiguous goals and unavoidable pathways. The way in which I intended the word 'system' to be understood is, however, much closer to what Ken Robinson himself refers to in terms of the artistic process: 'one of the functions of artistic processes is to give shape, form and coherence to our aesthetic experiences. The painter, poet, musician, and dancer, each works within different and symbolic modes, through the varying logics of which they attempt to formulate and express different aspects of perception – visual, verbal, aural, kinaesthetic'.

Ken Robinson was a major contributor to the Gulbenkian Foundations' Report *The Arts in Schools* (1982). Part of that report was concerned with the serious lack of balance in the curriculum: the arts and the aesthetic development of children being seriously neglected in most schools. The problem of how to put this right is probably too difficult to include in a single chapter, but the arguments are cogently put – and further detail is available – in the Gulbenkian Report itself. Every school should have a copy; every teacher should read it. Ken Robinson is now editor of *Arts Express*, a publication which deserves to be read by teachers.

Denis Lawton

The same thing, seen from different points of view, gives rise to two entirely different descriptions, and the descriptions give rise to two entirely different theories, and the theories result in two entirely different sets of action (Laing, 1965).

Most schools do not have a policy on the content and organisation of the curriculum nor on curriculum development. Given the competing political and educational pressures on the timetable, the need for such policies may seem obvious. One of the jobs of curriculum theory is to suggest organising principles for these policies. In this chapter I want to look at issues for curriculum development in aesthetic education. In doing so I want to question some prevailing assumptions about the content of the curriculum, and the idea of cultural systems as an alternative. This may have particular disadvantages for aesthetic education, for reasons which may well apply to other areas of curriculum planning.

What is Aesthetic Education?

It would be presumptuous in the space available, and with a number of other themes in front of us, to attempt to unravel the great complexities of aesthetic experience, or of the many theories which have been developed to explain them. The complexities are considerable, and we should here only make some brief but fundamental points of description before moving onto other and perhaps firmer ground.

'Aesthetic' has come to be used in a variety of ways and in a number of contexts. It is often used, wrongly, as a synonym for 'artistic'. Although the two ideas are related, as we shall see, they are distinguishable. 'Aesthetic' is also used of particular branches of practical criticism and of philosophical theory. In everyday language it is used more generally to suggest pleasing qualities or characteristics of events, or objects.

There are three fundamental observations to make about the concept of the 'aesthetic'. First, and for reasons we will come back to, aesthetic refers primarily not to qualities in events or objects, but to our perceptions of them. Second, aesthetic perceptions concern our pleasure in the form and presentation of events and objects. Third, aesthetic responses are not exclusive to any particular area of human experience. We may have aesthetic responses to mathematical theorems, to scientific proofs, iron bridges, poems or symphonies. This is because we have, as human beings, an innate capacity for aesthetic response which is integral to our general processes of perception and communication. The task of aesthetic education is to provide opportunities for this capacity to be exercised and developed. This is essential not because aesthetic experience is related to pleasure, and education should be more enjoyable –though it should; it is because the perception of beauty, aptness and significance in form is in itself a process of evaluation. Aesthetics, in a stricter sense, as Santayana (1955) puts it, is essentially concerned with the perception of values. Aesthetic education thus draws in moral education and the education of feeling and human sensibility. These are areas which have been almost entirely neglected in some schools. The weight of social evidence does not support the wisdom of letting this drift much further.

The Arts and Aesthetic Experience

We not only respond in aesthetic ways to objects and events we happen across, we are also driven to create objects of aesthetic contemplation. The arts – music, dance, drama, literature and the visual arts – are creative processes in which this capacity has special significance. We do not engage in the arts for aesthetic reasons alone. The arts are among the ways in which we formulate some of our most fundamental ideas and perceptions about ourselves and the worlds we live in, and through which we communicate these ideas to ourselves and to each other. What Marcuse (1979) calls 'the aesthetic dimension' is a defining characteristic of this process, but it is not the only one, nor is the giving or receiving of aesthetic pleasure the only, nor necessarily the prime, motive for engaging in the arts in the first place. An artist's motives may be explicitly didactic or political. In every case, artists are concerned with, and sometimes obsessed by, issues of perception and understanding. They work in their chosen art forms, because they find in them their greatest freedom and opportunity to articulate and communicate ideas and perceptions which would otherwise be literally inconceivable.

The arts do not exhaust our aesthetic capacities, nor do aesthetic interests entirely account for our involvement in the arts. Nevertheless, the arts do provide a specific focus for aesthetic capabilities. They have particular importance in this and other respects in the education of all children and young people. For this reason we want to develop the themes of this discussion in particular relation to the arts and to indicate areas of generalisation beyond them as we go on.

The Arts and Education

In the report of the Gulbenkian inquiry *The Arts in Schools* (1982) we drew together a number of key arguments for the necessity of providing adequately for the arts in education. We argued that this provision is essential:

1 in developing the full variety of human intelligence
2 in developing the capacity for creative thought and action
3 in the education of feeling and sensibility
4 in the exploration of values
5 in understanding cultural change and differences
6 in developing physical and perceptual skills.

In presenting these arguments we were aware of severe problems of curriculum development and implementation. These can be identified here as political ideological problems. Any school concerned to improve its provision for aesthetic education will need to take a view of these.

Political Problems

Many schools now face severe difficulties of resources in staff, materials and facilities. Two of the reasons for this are, first, the effects of economic retrenchment, and second, of falling rolls. The result in most cases has been cuts in services. In effecting these cuts schools and local education authorities have been compelled, sometimes for the first time, to identify educational priorities – though, tragically, this is being done not in a spirit of what should be developed first, but of what should be sacrificed last. A third reason, which is interacting with these two, is the cumulative effects of long term structural unemployment. Fearing the consequences of being unqualified in a shrinking labour market, parents and pupils are adding to the pressure on schools to concentrate on what they mistakenly[1] see as their best chance of survival – higher numbers of examination passes. In these circumstances, talk of aesthetic education may seem a little beside the point, though in an ominous development, the case for the arts has begun to be accepted by politicians who see a way out of their difficulties by talking at conferences about education for leisure.

We give some attention to these issues in the Gulbenkian report and so they will not be pursued here. It is important to register their significance, however, especially since they interact so closely with the equally serious ideological problems which face the arts in education.

Ideological Problems

Views on education, and of much else, are often not the expression of conscious analysis, but of unexamined ideology. Few people – including a number of educationalists – would claim to have or to hold an explicit theory of education. There is no reason – except in the case of educationalists – why they should. This does not stop people holding and expressing views on education, any more than it would stop them holding and expressing views on anything else. Formal theory consists of explicit patterns of ideas which are consciously and deliberately developed to illuminate experience. Ideology is often unrecognised; taking ideology to mean the inferential structures of values and beliefs which constitute for any person what Polanyi (1969) has called his/her tacit knowledge and understanding of the world. These act together to form what Schutz (1967 and 1972) describes as an individual's 'taken-for-granted' view of reality – his/her natural conception of the way things are.

For a long time it was assumed that the earth was flat. It looked flat, and there was no reason in common sense to think it was anything else. In this, as in many other instances, even hard evidence to the contrary and persuasive theories to back it up was not accepted immediately, nor without a great deal of opposition. After all, accepting such fundamental challenges to common sense can rock the very foundations on which our view of the world, and of our relations to it are founded.

Theory and ideology interact, however. We all now live, more or less, within the ideological structures which derive from the now proven theory, for most of us, that the world is actually round. In more recent times, our ideologies have gradually accommodated other equally cataclysmic theories – of Freud in psychoanalysis, Einstein in physics and Darwin in biology. Each of these, once tremendous outrages to common sense, are now coolly taken-for-granted as obvious and just the way things are.

Education has its own ideological planks. For some it is the common sense idea – hotly disputed by many theorists – that the purpose of education is to prepare young people for work. For many more it is probably just as obvious that the organising principle for the curriculum should be the evident existence of different 'subjects', and that the job of the teacher is to teach children about them. It is important to challenge this attitude here because it has its roots in a contestable ideology – which has many theories to support it – concerning the nature of knowledge. In a number of respects this ideology is hostile to the place we claim for the arts in education and to the value of aesthetic experience in general.

Developing the Individual

The state system of education was founded to meet the overtly instrumental aims of providing a literate and numerate workforce. The content of the curriculum was determined accordingly. Increasingly, educational theorists have argued that education should be seen not as a means to such extrinsic ends, but as an end in itself. The focus should be on developing the individual for its own sake. Liberal views of education have been influential throughout this century, particularly in teacher training. In schools, they have had less impact at secondary than at primary level where the demands of the economy are less intrusive.

Educators differ in their views of what an individual is and how to develop one. We can pick out as markers in this complex web of theories and ideologies two broad conceptions or paradigms of individualism, the *rational* and the *natural*.[2] These have quite different implications for curriculum and pedagogy. We will come back to the natural paradigm a little later.

The Rational Paradigm

Within the rational paradigm the individual is conceived of as possessing certain qualities of mind. The child becomes an autonomous individual by acquiring objective knowledge of the world and through organising and analysing his/her understanding of it through a disciplined process of rational thought. Two major influences on the development of the rational paradigm were the formulation in the seventeenth century of the principles of the inductive method in science, and of the empirical method in philosophy emerging from Descartes dualism of mind and matter.[3] For all their diversity in other ways, the methods developed in these traditions have two important characteristics in common.[4]

1 They assume the pre-eminent validity of discursive reason and of propositional knowledge.

2 They take for granted the necessity and the possibility of objective, defined as impersonal, procedures of inquiry.

In these traditions, which have dominated Western intellectual life since the seventeenth century, the pursuit of knowledge must accord with strict procedures of sequential reason. Feelings, intuitions, and especially emotions, are non-rational and potential sources of error. For, in the rational paradigm, knowledge is assumed to exist independently of people.

These procedures have been enormously beneficial, of course, in many areas of inquiry. The great adventures in science and technology since the Enlightenment bear eloquent witness to the power of this form of rationality. The difficulty is that they have sometimes come to be taken as the only measures of true knowledge in all realms of human experience. 'Scientism', as it is sometimes called, has led to the virtual exile of feeling and intuition and of other forms of knowing from intellectual life certainly in some schools. Ironically, this is despite theoretical developments in science and philosophy themselves[5] which aim to revise this attitude. As Louis Arnaud Reid (1981) has noted:

> . . . scientism (whatever its form) proclaims that science must be taken as the model for all that can properly claim to be 'knowledge'. Scientistic positivism, which has its roots in the history of empiricism, has been refuted long enough and as often pronounced dead. But it has refused to lie down. Perhaps, to change metaphors, it is nowadays more of an ideological assumption than an explicit belief, operating like a sort of virus in the blood stream in many people's – and not only in scientists' – minds.

The pervasive ideology of scientism in education is illustrated in the everyday references to 'scientific' and 'objective' tests, as the final court of appeal in matters of human assessment. Equally pervasive influences are the ideas of the subject and the fact. Louis Arnaud Reid again:

> . . . in the context of education one thing stands out. It is the domination, the almost exclusive domination, in the curriculum, of strictly 'public' and 'objective' knowledge . . . the acquisition of factual and conceptual knowledge which can to a considerable extent be impersonally tested and examined.

These educational ideologies are not without theoretical support. R. S. Peters (1973) writes, for example, that the essential feature of

education consists in 'experienced persons turning the eye outwards
to what is essentially independent of persons'. We should mark, he
says, 'the enormous importance of the *impersonal* content and
procedures which are enshrined in public traditions'. The job of the
teacher here is to initiate pupils into the different forms of public
knowledge. These provide the organising principle for the curriculum. Each has its own characteristic content, problems, and
rules of discourse. Paul Hirst (1969) writes of nine forms of
knowledge, or cognitive structures, each of which is overlapping but
contains unique and exclusive elements.

Although it would be wrong to equate rational individualism with
the academic tradition in British education, there is a clear accord
between the rationalist view and the structures and forms of
traditional, subject-based curricula. Since most of us were brought
up in the rationalist tradition, and since it seems so much like
common sense, the temptation is to take it for granted. There are
good reasons not to. The case for the practice and appreciation of the
arts is among them.

Personal Knowledge

Since the latter half of the nineteenth century, a body of theoretical
work has been building up which offers an altogether different view
of the processes of human knowledge and understanding. This has
important implications for education. The work is represented in the
writings of, for example, Susanne Langer (1951, 1953, 1964),
A. N. Whitehead (1927), Edmund Husserl (1958, 1970), Alfred
Schutz (1967, 1972), George Kelly (1963), Max Weber (1957),
William James (1980), Michael Polanyi (1969), Karl Popper
(1969), Ernst Cassirer (1953). Although there is considerable
dissidence between them over often fundamental matters – they are
in no sense a unified school of thought – they are identifiable as a
grouping because they have developed and share a number of
common assumptions about the nature of knowledge and of
knowing.

The first is that personal consciousness is not a passive receptacle
of impersonal knowledge, but that we actively invest meaning in our
experience of the world. Knowledge, in an important sense, is
personal. Second, knowledge evolves and changes through a
constant process of conjecture and communication between individuals and is both socially constructed and distributed.
Knowledge, in an important sense, is interpersonal.

In his study of *The Intelligence of Feeling*, Robert Witkin (1974) re-states the founding observation of modern Western philosophy, that the individual lives not in one world but in two.

> There is a world that exists beyond the individual, a world that exists whether or not he exists . . . There is another world, however, a world that exists only because he exists. It is the world of his own sensations and feelings. He shares the former world with others, for it is a world of facts, of public space of 'objects'. He shares the second world with no-one. It is the world of private space and the solitary subject.

We recognise the truth of this; that, as Laing (1965) puts it,

> We can only be ourselves in and through the world and that there is a sense in which 'our' world will die with us although 'the' world will go on without us.

The recognition of this distinction marks an important stage on the road to personal autonomy. In empirical terms, however, this common sense distinction begs the most important questions of all: how do we know the external world exists; how is our knowledge of it constituted; how can this knowledge be legitimised; how can we compare our knowledge to other people's, assuming they are there?

These questions have been of central interest not only in modern philosophy but increasingly in the emerging 'sociology of knowl-edge' and in particular to those writers, including some of those listed above, loosely labelled as phenomenologists and as symbolic interactionists.

Their analyses begin like Descartes from the assumption that the one certain basis for investigating knowledge is the process of the consciousness which is doing the thinking. Knowledge only exists where there are knowers. Moreover, public or shared knowledge is organised and communicated in patterns of symbols of various sorts. But a sign or symbol such as a word, a painting, an equation, or any pattern of these is sterile until it is brought to life in an act of personal understanding. A symbol means nothing unless its meaning is perceived and understood by a conscious intelligence. Into every act of knowing there enters 'a tacit and passionate contribution of the person knowing what is being known'. This personal element 'is no mere imperfection, but a necessary component of all knowledge' (Polanyi, 1969).

Many of the symbols we use we have organised into complex systems. The most pervasive of these is verbal language. It is within studies of language that the central implication of the use of symbols has been teased out: that we use symbols not only to communicate ideas about personal and shared experience, but actually to formulate them. In learning a language a child also learns the systems of relations and concepts of which the language principally consists – the structures of ideas within which he/she will be disposed to organise his/her understanding of experience. Learning the mother tongue plays a crucial part in the transmission of socially approved knowledge. As Schutz (1967) puts it:

> The native language can be taken as a set of references which . . . have pre-determined what features of the world are worthy of being expressed and what qualities of these features and what relations among them deserve attention.

For this reason, Karl Popper describes all language as being 'theory impregnated'. In learning a language the child learns a culture.

Finding Forms

Verbal language may be the most pervasive, but it is not the only, nor is it necessarily the most significant symbolism. Langer (1951) makes the crucial point that we use different modes of symbolism to formulate and express different forms and qualities of experience. Verbal language places one symbol after another in sequences which are governed by systematic rules of grammer and syntax. This does well for formulating discursive propositions. But some ideas and experiences simply will not go into words. Expressing them in this form is like stringing clothes which are worn one inside another on a washing line. For these non-discursive thoughts, we need, and we have developed, other modes of symbolism – including those of the expressive arts.

Ways of Knowing

This discussion began by saying that the arts are distinguishable from the aesthetic. They are. But one of the functions of artistic processes is to give shape, form and coherence to our aesthetic experiences. The painter, poet, musician, and dancer each works within different symbolic modes, through the varying logics of which they attempt to formulate and express different aspects of perception – visual, verbal, aural, kinaesthetic. A key feature of these modes is that they do not divorce thought and feeling, logic and intuition but reflect the crucial ways in which they are inseparable.

Some serious objections to the idea of knowledge being impersonal and confined to the discursive realm have been outlined already. These objections also confront the idea of bodies of knowledge as the basis for curriculum planning. Artists do not differ from each other in terms of the subject matter of their work. Nor do other disciplines. The subject matter of art is whatever happens to interest the artist. The same is true of science. What differs between disciplines is the mode of enquiry and the attitude in which it is conducted – the line of interest of the inquirer. The same phenomena can be investigated within different realms of meaning – mathematical, poetic, biological, musical. To this extent, it may be more fitting to think not of bodies of knowledge, but of ways of knowing. We are born with the potential to know the world in many different ways. It is education which has done so much to enforce one – no matter how valuable – to the virtual exclusion of the rest. The result, as we argued in *The Arts in Schools* is a serious imbalance in educational provision.

Is there an Aesthetic System?

Some criticisms of 'bodies of knowledge' as a basis for curriculum planning have been rehearsed here. It has been suggested that a more useful basis may be the idea of cultural systems, and that one of these might be 'the aesthetic system'. Cultural analysis has a good deal to recommend it in curriculum planning. 'Cultural systems' give some pause for thought.

Art is frequently referred to as a system. Polanyi, for example, places art among 'the great systems of utterance which try to evoke and impose correct modes of feeling' – science, religion, morality, law – 'and other constituents of culture' (Polanyi, 1969). Similarly, Berger and Luckman write of the 'immense edifices of symbolic representation that tower over the reality of everyday life', and add that 'religion, philosophy, art and science, are the historically most important systems of this kind' (Berger and Luckman, 1971). But is art a system?

Grotowski (1975) writing about the creative interpretation of the actor, director *and audience* observes that:

All great texts represent a sort of deep gulf for us. Take Hamlet.
Professors will tell us, each for himself, that they have discovered an
objective Hamlet. They suggest to us revolutionary Hamlets, rebel and
impotent Hamlets, Hamlet the outsider, etc. But there is no objective
Hamlet. The strength of great works really consists in their catalystic
effects: they open doors . . . '

We are familiar with the rival interpretations and theories of
literary and drama critics, of musical and artistic commentators. No
one would seriously expect to have these disagreements about the
meaning of works of art if their meanings were conveyed as
systematically as in scientific theories or technical diagrams. It has
been suggested here that the development and transmission of social
knowledge and culture is carried out through various forms of
symbolism. It may be useful to distinguish between three main forms
of symbolism: aformal, systematic and schematic.

Formal and Aformal Symbolism

Symbolism is not a special quality of a particular species of object or
event, but a function it serves. Some are devised specifically to serve
such a function – words, mathematical signs, paintings – others are
not, but are still perceived symbolically. Any object or event may
serve as a symbol for me by virtue of personal association, or my
subjective state in their presence. A sunset may represent melan-
choly or sublimity, just as a made object, a lamp or a pen, may be
steeped in significance known only to me. Such symbols are
personal, psychological and aformal.
     Formal symbols are those which we create intentionally. We can
distinguish broadly between those which are systematic and
schematic and suggest that the symbolism of the arts is of the second
type. Spoken and written language and mathematics are obvious
examples of systematic symbolisms in that they have:

1 separate elements which are definable in terms of each other
2 syntactical rules governing the relationships into which they can
  be meaningfully composed.

Such symbolisms are systematic to the extent that sense is clearly
divided from nonsense through agreed rules of discourse. We may
not be able to understand what a given proposition means, but we
can generally recognise that it makes sense because it conforms to the
logic of the system; and if we meet a new word we can always look it
up. But as I have noted elsewhere (1980):

If we want to understand the meaning of a painting we cannot turn to a dictionary of colours or a grammar of visual forms to see what blue and green mean when they are put together. There is no manual of significance to tell us what a sonata is driving at, and no dramatic taxonomy will decode a play for us. There is no fixed usage for the symbolism of art which divides sense from nonsense.

Works of art are complex, unique schematic symbols created out of a sense of essential form rather than of conventional usage. The artist creates these forms through a reflexive process of expression in which the forms emerge through exploring the particular issues at hand. This process is necessary because the artist is dealing with always more than, and often other than, propositional knowledge.

Schematic symbols may be created out of systemic symbols. Plays are written in words and there is a system of musical notation. But the score is not the music, and the text is not the play. These are the forms in which the schematic symbols are encoded and from which their meaning must be apprehended. Artists may work systematically and may follow certain professional conventions. But in the cultures of the industrialised West at least there are no general rules of artistic symbolism and discourse to justify the claim that there is an aesthetic system.

There are two other difficulties with the idea of cultural systems as a basis for curriculum planning. The first is that the concept itself owes so much to the discursive, propositional conception of knowledge to which we have been considering more broadly based alternatives. This is not to say that there are no cultural systems, but that not all cultural manifestations can be pressed into this particular conceptual mould. Second, and related to this, in undertaking a cultural analysis it will be important to distinguish between categories of cultural experience: for example, between the *transactional systems* – those which concern the material interactions and social maintenance of a culture – such as its technologies and economics, and the personal *perceptual processes*, such as the aesthetic, through which the individual makes sense of the culture.

The interactions within and between these are considerable. Legal systems, for example, are to some degree a projection of moral codes, which reciprocate with systems of belief. Williams (1971) has argued, for example, for closer examinations of the patterns of industrial development and changes in forms of democratic government, their cumulative effects on the shape of communities and the organisation and content of education. These 'long revolutions' in industry and democracy are also enmeshed in a broader cultural revolution which in turn is being interpreted 'and

indeed fought out in very complex ways in the world of art and ideas'
(Williams, 1971). The analysis of culture is not the study of separate
areas of social activity – as in the subject-based curriculum – but of
the *relationships* between the various processes of social life.

The Individual Pupil and the Pupal Individual

Two paradigms of individualsim were referred to earlier, the
rational and the natural, and we promised to come back to the
second. Natural individualism developed to some extent as a
reaction to rationalism. It has it recent roots in eighteenth century
Romanticism and in the writings of Rousseau (1911), Froebel
(1909), Montessori (1912), and Dewey (1931). This paradigm is also
focused on the individual, but it argues that children are born as
individuals and should be allowed the space in which to grow.
Education should follow a natural pattern of personal development
rather than a standard course of instruction. Like a sculptor the
teacher is encouraged to follow the inherent grain of the child's
personality, slowly revealing the individual within.

In terms of our analysis so far, this model has much to commend it.
Teachers in this tradition show a characteristic concern with 'the
whole child', with encouraging the expression of feelings and
emotions and with the development of the imagination. It does share
one significant deficiency with the rationalist attitude. It presents a
view of individual development which is asocial. Both ignore the
extent to which the development of the individual is affected by and
reciprocates with the values, attitudes and mores of the social culture
of which he/she is part. The danger for the arts in this approach, as
Polanyi (1969) has intimated, is that however expressive and
individual children's activities may seem to be, unless their critical
and evaluative powers are deliberately encouraged they may simply
be expressing values they have inherited and emotions they have
been taught to feel. The point of an education in the arts is to enable
the individual to reflect critically on and to evaluate their experiences of and in the social culture.

The Arts and Cultural Education

If arts teachers in the rationalist tradition tend to teach children
about the arts, their naturalist colleagues sometimes eschew participation and critical studies altogether on the grounds that this is

an irrelevant distraction for children who should be getting on with their own work. On the basis of this discussion both views are mistaken and provide no basis for pupil or curriculum development.

The idea of education through the arts implies children using them to formulate and present their own feelings and ideas. The importance of this is in enabling them to become what Freire (1976) calls meaning-givers rather than just meaning-takers. Any historical epoch, according to Freire has characteristic themes and concerns. Whether or not individuals can perceive these themes,

> . . . and above all how they act on the reality within which these themes are generated will largely determine their humanisation or dehumanisation, their affirmation as subjects or their reduction as objects. For only as they grasp the themes can they intervene in reality instead of remaining merely onlookers.

Engaging practically in the arts is among the ways that children can become active and creative participants in the social culture. Realised works of art are among the key features of the social culture with which, in trying to make sense of it, children need to engage. Works of art have particular significance because of their distinctive roles in perception and understanding. This process can also provide both the fuel and ignition for children's own further work and development through the arts.

In the general context of curriculum planning, these reciprocal elements in aesthetic education are among the ways of acting on Archbishop Temple's call to teach people to feel together and to think for themselves, instead of thinking together and feeling alone.

NOTES

1 For a full discussion of this issue see, for example, Dore (1976).
2 For an interesting discussion of the concept of individualism see Hargreaves (1980).
3 Two major influences on the evolution of the rational paradigm were the formulation of the principles of the inductive method, as set down in the seventeenth century by Francis Bacon, and subsequently by John Stuart Mill, and of the empirical method in philosophy emerging from Descartes' *cogito*.
4 The empiricism of an inductive scientist is rather different from that of a post-Cartesian philosopher. As Susanne Langer (1951) has noted, where Cartesian empiricism was essentially sceptical and sought to question the evidence of the senses, scientific empiricism became increasingly positivist and took such evidence as its raw material.
5 See for example, Popper (1969) and Polanyi (1969).

10 School-based Curriculum Planning

Denis Lawton

So far the discussion of curriculum planning in this book has been at the fairly general level. We have tried to outline what we think should be offered to all young people, 5 to 16, under the headings of the eight cultural systems. This would be the basis of planning a common curriculum nationally. But a common curriculum is not a uniform curriculum. Whilst all young people should have a right to be offered certain curriculum experiences, *how* it is made available will vary from one school to another, depending partly on how that school is organised, including the teachers available, and partly on the local environment and particular needs of the children in that school.

Having decided on a particular model of curriculum planning, the next stage for the school will be to decide how to convert general guidelines into a set of school syllabuses. No book can achieve this task for the teachers in a school. The final process of curriculum planning must be undertaken as a process of discussion among those teachers involved in trying to plan a better curriculum. But there are certain procedures which many schools have found helpful. One of these is the very simple approach of matrix planning.

A matrix approach can be used at a number of different levels in the task of school curriculum planning. At the most general level it may be useful to start with a list of existing subjects at the top of the matrix, and the eight cultural systems down the left hand side. An early discussion among the teachers involved in curriculum planning groups would identify what each subject had to offer in any of the eight systems, bearing in mind the kind of 'content' suggested for each cultural system in Chapters 2 to 9 of this book.

This approach has two advantages. First its prevents the 'deskilling' of the teachers, avoiding the problems created by requiring history teachers to teach the geography needed in a humanities

Figure 3

Existing Subjects

Cultural systems	English	Maths	Science	Religious Education	History	Geography	Modern Languages	Art	Music	Physical Education	Craft, Design and Technology	Home Economics
1 Socio-political												
2 Economic												
3 Communication												
4 Rationality												
5 Technology												
6 Morality												
7 Belief												
8 Aesthetic												

course, for example; instead, this approach asks the positive question 'what can you offer under this heading?'. The second advantage is that it is also possible at this stage to identify gaps: either completely empty lines on the matrix, for example, if no teacher feels competent to say anything at all about the economic system, or, more likely, that although several subjects feel that they have something to offer in the morality system, that the existing offerings would not add up to a coherent curriculum policy for the school. In both cases, painful and difficult decisions might be necessary: perhaps, finding some volunteers to undertake retraining in economics, in the first case; discussing how best to provide useful teaching materials to supplement the existing offerings in the second case. It will not be easy, and it is foolish to pretend that a major task of curriculum planning can be undertaken without additional resources, including a considerable programming of in-service education for teachers on a regular basis.

A second use for the matrix approach is within any one cultural system. In Chapter 2, for example, Richard Whitburn has suggested under the heading of General Political Concepts that pupils need to gain understanding of the following: power, authority, welfare, freedom, liberty. Having identified, by means of the first matrix exercise, which subjects teachers are willing to 'offer' in this area, it will now be possible to use another matrix at a different level as a planning technique to work out a possible 'division of labour'.

Figure 4   **Subjects involved**

Concepts	History	Geography	English	Religious Education
power				
authority				
welfare				
freedom				
liberty				

At this stage, if not earlier, it will be necessary to appoint a co-ordinator for each of the eight cultural systems. It would then become the responsibility of a co-ordinator to achieve a coherent programme for each school year, and that each year's programme would eventually add up to a coherent programme for the school as a whole, for the age group 5 to 11, or 11 to 16, or whatever was the relevant age group for that particular school.

It will be observed that once we get beyond seeing school subjects as ends in themselves, then the task of curriculum planning becomes an elaborate matching exercise. If subjects are seen as means to more general cultural purposes, a school-based curriculum is forged out of a match between what subject teachers can offer and what is regarded as a set of essential learning experiences for the pupils. Because the curriculum guidelines begin with assumptions or statements about what all young people need, the approach could be described as child-centred. But the curriculum planning exercise begins by asking what teachers have to offer; in this sense all school-based curriculum planning is necessarily teacher-centred.

Bibliography

ASHTON, P. *et al.* (1975) *The Aims of Primary Education: a study in teachers' opinions.* Schools Council, London: Macmillan.

ASHTON, P. *et al.* (1975) *Aims into Practice in the Primary School.* Schools Council, London: Hodder and Stoughton.

BALDWIN, J. and WELLS, H. (1979) *Active Tutorial Work 1–5.* Oxford: Basil Blackwell.

BARLEY, C. (1980) 'Morality, reason and feeling', *Journal of Moral Education*, **9**, 2.

BARNES, D. (1971) 'Language and Learning in the Classroom', *Journal of Curriculum Studies*, **3**, 1.

BARNES, D., BRITTON, J. and ROSEN, H. (1969, revised 1971) *Language, the Learner and the School.* London: Penguin.

BARNES, D. and TODD, F. (1977) *Communication and Learning in Small Groups.* London: Routledge and Kegan Paul.

BERGER, P. L. and LUCKMAN, T. (1971) *The Social Construction of Reality.* London: Penguin.

BLATT, M. and KOHLBERG, L. (1975) 'The effects of classroom moral discussion upon children's level of moral judgement', *Journal of Moral Education*, **4**, 2.

BOARD OF EDUCATION (1943) *Educational Reconstruction.* London: HMSO.

BOYSON, R. (1978) 'There is more to life than learning about politics' *The Times* 31/1/1978.

BRITISH FILM INSTITUTE (1981) Report on Media Education Conference. London: BFI.

BRITISH HUMANIST ASSOCIATION (1975) *Objective, Fair and Balanced.* London: BHA.

BRYDEN-BROOK, S. (1972) 'Moral studies in the secondary school', *Journal of Moral Education*, **1**, 2.

BULL, N. J. (1973) *The Way of Wisdom, 1–4.* Amersham: Hulton Educational.

BUTTON, L. (1974) *Developmental Group Work with Adolescents.* London: Hodder and Stoughton.

BUTTON, L. (1981, 1982) *Group Tutoring for the Form Teacher: 1 Lower Secondary School, 2 Upper Secondary School.* London: Hodder and Stoughton.

CASSIRER, E. (1953) *The Philosophy of Symbolic Forms, Volume 1: Language.* New Haven, Connecticut: Yale University Press.

CHESTON, M. (1979) *It's Your Life.* Exeter: Wheaton.

CHRISTIAN EDUCATION MOVEMENT (1983) *Religious and Moral Education in Inner City Schools.* London: CEM.

COX, E. (1983) *Problems and Possibilities for Religious Education.* London: Hodder and Stoughton.

CRICK, B. and PORTER, A. (1980) *Political Education and Political Literacy.* London: Longman.

CROSS, M. (1982) *Moral Values – classroom practice and school planning.* St Martin's College, Lancaster.

DAVIES, H. R. H. (1972) *The Root of the Matter.* London: Edward Arnold.

DEARDEN, R. F. (1968) *The Philosophy of Primary Education.* London: Routledge and Kegan Paul.

DEARDEN, R. F. (1981) 'Balance and coherence', *Cambridge Journal of Education*, **2**, 2.

DEARDEN, R. F., HIRST, P. H, and PETERS, R. S. (eds) (1972) *Education and the Development of Reason.* London: Routledge and Kegan Paul.

DEFORGE (1972) *The Teaching of Technology.* Strasbourg: Council of Europe.

DEPARTMENT OF EDUCATION AND SCIENCE (1975) *A Language for Life* (The Bullock Report). London: HMSO.

DEPARTMENT OF EDUCATION AND SCIENCE (1977a) *Education in Schools: A Consultative Document* (Green Paper). London: HMSO.

DEPARTMENT OF EDUCATION AND SCIENCE (1977b) *Curriculum 11–16.* London: HMSO.

DEPARTMENT OF EDUCATION AND SCIENCE (1978) *Special Educational Needs* (The Warnock Report). London: HMSO.

DEPARTMENT OF EDUCATION AND SCIENCE (1978) *Primary Education in England: a Survey by H. M. Inspectors of Schools*. London: HMSO.

DEPARTMENT OF EDUCATION AND SCIENCE (1979) *Aspects of Secondary Education in England: a Survey by H. M. Inspectors of Schools*. London: HMSO.

DEPARTMENT OF EDUCATION AND SCIENCE (1980a) *A View of the Curriculum*. London: HMSO.

DEPARTMENT OF EDUCATION AND SCIENCE (1980b) *A Framework for the School Curriculum*. London: HMSO.

DEPARTMENT OF EDUCATION AND SCIENCE (1981a) *The School Curriculum*. London: HMSO.

DEPARTMENT OF EDUCATION AND SCIENCE (1981b and onwards) *Assessment of Performance Unit, Language Performance in Schools, Primary and Secondary Reports*. London: HMSO.

DEPARTMENT OF EDUCATION AND SCIENCE (1982a) *Education 5–9: an illustrative survey of 80 first schools in England*. London: HMSO.

DEPARTMENT OF EDUCATION AND SCIENCE (1982b) *17+: A New Qualification*. London: HMSO.

DEPARTMENT OF EDUCATION AND SCIENCE (1983a) *9–13 Middle Schools: an illustrative survey*. London: HMSO.

DEPARTMENT OF EDUCATION AND SCIENCE (1983b) *Popular Television and Schoolchildren*. London: HMSO.

DEPARTMENT OF EDUCATION AND SCIENCE (1985) *The Curriculum from 5 to 16*. London: HMSO.

DEWEY, J. (1931) *Individualism: Old and New*. London: Allen and Unwin.

DINGWALL, R. (1971) *Relationships*. Exeter: Religious and Moral Education Press.

DOMNITZ, M. (1971) *Strides in Human Relationships*. Oxford: Pergamon.

DORE, R. (1976) *The Diploma Disease*. London: Unwin Education.

FREIRE, P. (1976) *Education: The Practice of Freedom*. London: Writers and Readers.

FROEBEL, F. (1909) *The Education of Man* (trans. Hailmann, W. N.) New York: Appleton.

GARDINER, T. (1984) *Thinking for Life*. London: Edward Arnold.

GORDON, P. and LAWTON, D. (1978) *Curriculum Change in the Nineteenth and Twentieth Centuries*. London: Hodder and Stoughton.

GRAINGER, A. J. (1970) *The Bullring Classroom Experiment*. Oxford: Pergamon.

GROTOWSKI, J. (1975) *Towards a Poor Theatre*. London: Methuen.

GULBENKIAN (1982) *The Arts in Schools: Principles, Practice and Provision*. London: Calooste Gulbenkian Foundation.

HAMILTON, J. (1982) *Education in an Industrial Society*, Shell Lecture.

HANSARD SOCIETY (1978) *Programme for Political Education*. London: Hansard Society.

HARGREAVES, D. H. (1980) *A Sociological Critique of Individualism in Education*. Mimeo. University of Oxford, Department of Educational Studies.

HARRISON, G. (1981) 'The British Technic', Stanley Lecture.

HEMMING, J. (1980) 'Another prospect on moral education', *Journal of Moral Education*, **9**, 2.

HIRST, P. H. (1969) 'The Logic of the Curriculum', *Journal of Curriculum Studies*, **1**, 2.

HIRST, P. H. (1973) 'Religion: a form of knowledge? A Reply', *Learning for Living*, **12**, 4.

HOLLEY, B. and SKELTON, V. (1980) *Economics Education 14–16 Phase One: Final Report*. London : NFER.

INNER LONDON EDUCATION AUTHORITY (1983) *History and Social Sciences at Secondary Level, Part Three: Social Sciences*. London: ILEA.

JAMES, W. (1980) *The Principles of Psychology*. New York: Holt.

JONES, C. (1976a) 'The contribution of history and literature to moral education', *Journal of Moral Education*, **5**, 2.

JONES, C. (1976b) 'The contribution of science to moral education', *Journal of Moral Education*, **5**, 3.

KELLY, G. (1963) *A Theory of Personality*. New York : Norton.

KOHLBERG, L. (1981) *Essays on Moral Development, Vol. 1*. Cambridge, MA: Harvard University Press.

KRESS, G. (1983) *Learning to Write*. London: Routledge and Kegan Paul.

KROLL, B. and VANN, D. J. (1981) *Exploring speaking-writing relationships, connections and contrasts*. London: NCTE.

LADENBURG, T. and M. and SCHARF, P. (1978) *Moral Education – a classroom workbook based on Kholberg*. Davis, CA: Responsible Action.

LAING, R. D. (1965) *The Divided Self*. London: Penguin.
LANGER, S. K. (1951) *Philosophy in a New Key*. New York: New American Library.
LANGER, S. K. (1953) *Feeling and Form*. London: Routledge and Kegan Paul.
LANGER, S. K. (1964) *Philosophical Sketches*. New York: New American Library.
LAWTON, D. (1983) *Curriculum Studies and Educational Planning*. London: Hodder and Stoughton.
LUNZER, E. A. and GARDNER, K. (1979) *The Effective Use of Reading*. London: Heinemann.
LUSTED, D. and DRUMMOND, P. (1985) *Television and Schooling*. London: British Film Institute.
MACAULEY, W. J. (1947) 'The Difficulty of Grammar', *British Journal of Educational Psychology*, 17.
MACINTYRE, A. (1978) Review of *Introduction to Moral Education*, *New Society*, 29/2/1968.
MCPHAIL, P. (1981) *Social and Moral Education*. Oxford: Basil Blackwell.
MCPHAIL, P., UNGOED-THOMAS, J. and CHAPMAN, H. (1972a) *Moral Education in the Secondary School*. London: Longman.
MCPHAIL, P., UNGOED-THOMAS, J. and CHAPMAN, H. (1972b) *Lifeline*. London: Longman.
MCPHAIL, P., UNGOED-THOMAS, J. and CHAPMAN, H. (1978) *Startline*. London: Longman.
MACY, C. (1969) *Let's Teach Them Right*. London: Pemberton Books.
MALEY (1983) Unpublished paper. University of Maryland.
MANPOWER SERVICES COMMISSION (1984) *TVEI Review*. Sheffield: MSC.
MARCUSE, H. (1979) *The Aesthetic Dimension*. London: Macmillan.
MARTIN, C. G. (1973) *It's Up to You*. Amersham: Hulton Educational.
MATTHEWS, D. (1977) *The Reference of School Leaving Experience of Performance in Industry*. Stockport: Engineering Industry Training Board.
MAY, P. R. (1971) *Moral Education in Schools*. London: Methuen.
MONTESSORI, M. (1912) *The Montessori Method*, London: Heinemann.
MOSHER, R. L. and SULLIVAN, P. R. (1976) 'A curriculum in moral education for adolescents', *Journal of Moral Education*, **5**, 2.
NATIONAL ASSOCIATION FOR TEACHING OF ENGLISH (1976) *Language Across the Curriculum: Guidelines for Schools*. NATE.
NOTTINGHAM, B. and CROSS, M. (1981) *Moral Education Across the Curriculum*. St Martin's College, Lancaster.
PARRINDER, G. (1973) *Themes for Living, 1–4*. Amersham: Hulton Educational.
PAYAN, A (1972) 'The teaching of technology in France', *The Teaching of Technology*. Strasbourg: Council of Europe.
PETERS, R. S. (1961) 'Moral Education and the Psychology of Character', A paper read at the Harvard Graduate School of Education, 5/1961.
PETERS, R. S. (1973) *Authority, Responsibility and Education*. London: Allen and Unwin.
PETERSON, A. D. C. (ed.) (1965) *Techniques of Teaching*. Oxford: Pergamon.
PHENIX, P. (1964) *Realms of Meaning: A philosophy of the curriculum for general education*. New York: McGraw-Hill.
POLANYI, M. (1958, 1969) *Personal Knowledge: towards a post-critical philosophy*. London: Routledge and Kegan Paul.
POPPER, K. (1969) *Conjectures and Refutations: The growth of scientific knowledge*. London: Routledge and Kegan Paul.
PRING, R. (1984) *Personal and Social Education in the Curriculum*. London: Hodder and Stoughton.
REID, L. A. (1981) 'Art: feeling and knowing', *Journal of Philosophy of Education*, **15**, 1.
RICH, J. M. (1980) 'Moral education and the emotions', *Journal of Moral Education*, **9**, 2.
RICHARDSON, R. and CHAPMAN, J. (1971) *Frontiers of Enquiry*. London: Hart Davis Educational.
ROBINSON, K. (1980) *Exploring Theatre and Education*. London: Heinemann.
ROUSSEAU, J. J. (1911) *Emile* (trans. Foxley, B.). London: Dent.
RUDDOCK, J. (1976) *Dissemination of Innovation: The Humanities Curriculum Project* (War and Society; Education; Family; Relations between the sexes; People at work; Poverty; Law and order; Living in cities). London: Evans/Methuen.
SANTAYANA (1955) *The Sense of Beauty*. New York: Dover.

SCHUTZ, A. (1967) *Collected Papers 1: The Problem of Social Reality*. The Hague: Martinus Nijhoff.

SCHUTZ, A. (1972) *The Phenomenology of the Social World* (trans. Walsh, G. and Lehnert, F.). London: Heinemann.

SCHOOLS COUNCIL (1981) *The Practical Curriculum*. London: Methuen.

SCOTTISH EDUCATION DEPARTMENT (1980) *Learning and Teaching in P4 and P7*. London: HMSO.

SEARLE, A. (1971) 'A study of admired people among adolescents in relation to aggression and sex differences', *Journal of Moral Education*, **1**, 1.

SIMON, S. B. (1972) *Values Clarification. A Handbook*. New York: Hart Publications.

SIMON, A. and WARD, L. O. (1973) 'Variables influencing pupils' responses on the Kohlberg schema of moral development', *Journal of Moral Education*, **2**, 3.

SINCLAIR, J. and COULTHARD, R. M. (1975) *Towards an Analysis of Discourse: English Used by Teachers and Pupils*. Oxford: Oxford University Press.

SKILBECK, M. (ed.) (1984) *Evaluating the Curriculum in the Eighties*. London: Hodder and Stoughton.

STUBBS, M. (1983) *Discourse Analysis*. Oxford: Basil Blackwell.

STUBBS, M. and DELAMONT, S. (eds.) (1976) *Explorations in Classroom Observation*. Chichester: John Wiley.

SUTTON, C. (1981) *Communicating in the Classroom*. London: Hodder and Stoughton.

THOMAS, L. M. (1981) *An Investigation of Economics Understanding Among Pupils Aged 12–16 Years*. Unpublished PhD thesis, University of London.

WARD, L. O. (1969) *Teaching Moral Values*. Exeter: Religious and Moral Education Press.

WARD, L. O. (1975) 'History–Humanity's Teacher?', *Journal of Moral Education*, **4**, 2.

WARD, L. O. (ed.) (1982) *The Ethical Dimension of the School Curriculum*. Pineridge Press.

WEBER, M. (1957) *The Theory of Social and Economic Organisation*: New York: Free Press.

WELLS, C. G. (1978) 'Talking with children: the complementary roles of parents and teachers', *English in Education*, **12**, 2.

WELLS, C. G. (1979) 'Describing children's linguistic development at home and at school,' *British Educational Research Journal*, **5**.

WHITE, J. (1973) *Towards a Compulsory Curriculum*. London: Routledge and Kegan Paul.

WHITEHEAD, A. N. (1927) *Symbolism: Its Meaning and Effects*. London: Macmillan.

WHITNEY, O. and E. (1970) *The Nature of Caring*. Oxford: Pergamon.

WILLIAMS, R. (1971) *The Long Revolution*. London: Penguin.

WILSON, J. (1969) *Moral Education and the Curriculum*. Oxford: Pergamon.

WILSON, J. (1971) *Education in Religion and Emotions*. London: Heinemann.

WILSON, J. (1972) *Practical Methods of Moral Education*. London: Heinemann.

WILSON, J. (1973a) *A Teacher's Guide to Moral Education*. London: Geoffrey Chapman.

WILSON, J. (1973b) *The Assessment of Morality*. London: NFER.

WILSON, J. (1972) *Ideals*. Cambridge: Lutterworth.

WILSON, J., WILLIAMS, N. and SUGARMAN, B. (1967) *An Introduction to Moral Education*. London: Penguin.

WITKIN, R. W. (1974) *The Intelligence of Feeling*. London: Heinemann.

WRIGHT, R. S. (ed.) (1972, 1973) *Asking them Questions, 1–2*. Oxford: Oxford University Press.

ZIMAN, J. (1976) *The Force of Knowledge: the scientific dimension of society*. Cambridge: Cambridge University Press.

ZIMAN, J. (1978) *Reliable Knowledge: an exploration of the grounds for belief in science*. Cambridge: Cambridge University Press.

ZIMAN, J. (1980) *Teaching and Learning about Science and Society*. Cambridge: Cambridge University Press.

Index